CONQUERING
THE
DECISION
ABYSS

TURNING DATA INTO ACTION IN
THE MODERN SUPPLY CHAIN

CONQUERING

THE

DECISION
ABYSS

KEITH HARTLEY

Keith Hartley
Alamo, California

Library of Congress Control Number: 9798998939716

Paperback ISBN: 979-8-9989397-1-6
eBook ISBN: 979-8-9989397-0-9

Book cover design by theBookDesigners
Interior design by theBookDesigners
Editorial production by KN Literary Arts

www.theabyssgroup.net

For Elsa and Mikaela,

Your laughter and courage inspire me each day to keep riding

life's waves with joy and purpose. Carpe punctum!

CONTENTS

FOREWORD

by ANGEL MENDEZ

In September of 1982, I was fortunate enough to be selected for General Electric's elite Manufacturing Management Program (MMP). I walked into the company's Consumer Electronics Division factory in Portsmouth, Virginia, excited to take on my very first job out of college. The role was for a Supplier Quality Engineer for electronic components, which meant I was responsible for developing incoming inspection and testing plans for all inbound parts used in GE's line up of televisions, VCRs, and video cameras. My role was to ensure that all components that crossed our incoming material dock were of the right quality before they could be released for production to the plant's manufacturing lines. At a high level, that may seem like no big deal. Make sure the parts work before they get assembled. As any of us in the supply chain know, however, things are never that easy or straightforward.

Back then GE's MMP program didn't come with any rookie training. This was a "jump into the pond and either sink or swim" type of program. I had trained in college as an Electrical Engineer, so my first instinct was to get my hands on as much data as I could. It was data that could help me to understand the scope of my responsibilities and organize my work. I needed to know things like what commodities I was responsible for, what suppliers I should care about, and what part numbers went into what product. I wanted the data to understand the quality results the company was already experiencing for the parts I was responsible for and the goals or metrics they were looking to achieve. I needed information on their existing inspection and testing processes and what the result was when failures occurred. I needed information on how those failures informed inspection plans.

Having this data would help me learn which suppliers were performing and which weren't. Perhaps most importantly, I wanted to understand the cost of bad quality. What would it mean to the organization when product parts failed? Given my lack of experience and the inability to leverage formal training, my first move was to ask my boss these questions. I was quickly reminded that as a graduate of an "elite college" and having been accepted into the MMP Program, his expectation was for me to fend for myself and deliver immediate improvements to all Key Performance Indicators. OK then. It was time to swim.

My next move was to ask an "old-timer" in the office, someone who knew his way around and understood the ins and outs of many of the roles in the department. Rich was my guy. He was a thirty-year veteran of that office, so I figured he'd surely lend me a hand. A man of few words, Rich was known as the "mechanicals and plastics" guy. He made it quite evident early into our interaction that he had little time to spare for the "MMP kid."

Rich's solution was to quickly point me to a room full of filing cabinets and wish me luck. After some meandering, I found what was referred to as "The Quality Room" in the back of the plant. It was filled with row after row of grey, metal filing cabinets organized by part category. Semiconductors had their own cabinet. There was another one for power supplies, and another for passive components. Each cabinet was further categorized by assigning parts of the drawer into part sub-categories. Within each drawer were files for each vendor. Inside them were files with Part and Quality Information Sheets (PQIS) for each part purchased from that vendor. The pieces of paper and lines of data seemed endless.

This ocean of compartmentalized data made me feel incompetent, until I found some of the valuable, useful information I was looking for buried among the records. My feelings of incompetence quickly shifted to feeling like the resident expert of GE parts. Nobody else was going through these files. That meant that nobody else in the building could possibly learn anything about component quality, or about what vendors to choose, or the cost of defects, or the root cause of quality problems. If they wanted answers, they had to directly collaborate with me. I found the data and I owned the data. I remember feeling quite smug about all that power. I learned that data meant influence. Data drove decision making. I held the data.

It didn't take long for me to realize the issues that all of this data presented, though. I learned that my biggest challenge was not the information I had, but the information I didn't have. I knew what the parts were and who supplied them, but I had no idea when those parts were coming into our receiving dock and how many we'd receive. Without this timing knowledge, I had no idea how to predict my workload or that of our inspectors. I also had no idea what each of the parts cost. This limited me from helping procurement perform any tradeoff analysis.

This issue became even worse when it came to new products that GE was developing. I had no idea what parts were expected to be used in new products, so I couldn't proactively build inspection plans or help design engineering decide which parts were best to consider for future designs. My quality inspections were reactive when parts showed up. Sometimes inspectors sat idly. Sometimes I didn't have the resources to help me manage the latest parts arrival.

I had plenty of data to work with, but what caused me the most technical issues was the data that I didn't have. Even with feeling like I had the keys to my data kingdom, I found myself feeling constantly surprised and ineffective. I had data, but I didn't have the right data to help me solve the problems in front of me. So I, like many others who have worked in some part of the supply chain, realized that I would just have to scramble and hustle every time something happened. I was always trying to figure things out.

Fast forward to today, forty years later. I would like to say that things have become exponentially better for supply chain professionals, but the reality is that they haven't. There is still so much scrambling and hustling to solve problems. While supply chain data has become digitized, it still retains the same compartmentalized and disparate organization in our cloud-enabled world as it did back when I was leafing through the multitude of filing cabinets. Those cabinets have now been replaced by ERP systems modules, data lakes, Excel spreadsheets, Google Drive, and SharePoint files.

This disparate data problem is no secret, but the right solution has still been elusive. Instead we've patched asymmetric information with Tableau tools and point software solutions that don't truly solve cross-functional interactions, deliver agility, or impart resilience. Practitioners have built new tools in an attempt to fill organizational data divides, knowledge gaps, and timing differences. The current solutions may work when things are going smoothly for the company, but in the world of sourcing and supply chain management that state of ease is only temporary.

Supply chain disruptions are a very real and very common occurrence, and our systems are struggling to keep up. What we now see defining the modern-day supply chain are those companies who can adapt to sourcing disruptions and those who can't. Like a boxing tournament, each round we lose manufacturers who can't compete with the bigger and stronger companies. We're no longer comparing filing cabinets to filing cabinets; now the companies with the deepest pockets to invest in technology or absorb the blow of supply chain disruptions are often the ones that survive until the next round. In the process, though, we are losing plenty of great smaller and newer innovators in manufacturing.

When I look back on my career, I'm glad I had the MMP program to force me into exploring new ways to do things.

Back then I had the flexibility and time to really dig deeper into the data at my disposal—data intelligence that was key to identifying problems and improving the cost savings of my company. The time and space to do that was a luxury that sourcing professionals in today's market can no longer enjoy. The pace is much quicker. There is an overwhelming amount of digital data, far more than our filing cabinets could have ever held, and yet we still lack the tools that effectively help us to identify and use this data to make informed decisions for each inevitable supply chain shock. They're best bet is that they can find an "old-timer" in their own office to help make sense of all of the spreadsheets and supplier relationships. But, is that really how we *want* to continue to operate? Is that the *best* way forward in this new world of data overwhelm and technological disconnect?

I am grateful that Keith Hartley set out to have this very necessary discussion in this book. Informed by many years of supply chain experience, Keith starts us on the path to solutions by clearly describing today's challenges and outlining how manufacturers can pull themselves out of this information abyss. As supply chain orchestration and agentic AI take hold across the modern supply chain practice, Keith reminds us of the importance of data context, concurrence, and collaboration enablement. These "first principles" must be addressed for the promise of AI-powered agility, resilience, and autonomy, contemporary aspirations of every supply chain practitioner, to become real. *Conquering the Decision Abyss* offers us both a call to action and a hopeful roadmap against a backdrop of an increasingly complex and disruptive business environment. Its insights are particularly important to newer or fast-growing manufacturers that need to make sense of their ever-expanding data sources, in a way that is both scalable and cost effective. It also challenges us to think about ourselves: the way we work and why we may be resistant to change, particularly as it relates to sourcing. We have to ask ourselves if we can, or even have the option to, continue operating as we do in the face of a rapidly-changing procurement landscape.

Conquering the Decision Abyss should be mandatory reading for every modern-day supply chain practitioner. It's the conversation we can no longer afford to avoid.

Angel Mendez
Chairman of the Board, LevaData

INTRODUCTION

"You're going to write a book?"

"Yep."

"On...what did you say it was?"

"Contextualizing data for sourcing professionals."

"Sounds riveting," she smirked before taking a sip of her coffee.

"It will be," I said, leaning back against our kitchen countertop. "This is the sourcing conversation that the supply chain industry needs to be having right now."

"I believe you."

Over our twenty-five years together, my wife, Bryn, has grown quite accustomed to me going after ambitious projects that seem to come out of left field. There was that time I built a sailboat before I knew how to sail one. There's my more recent hobby of brewing beer, even though I'm not much of a beer drinker myself. Call it a niggle or a wild hair, but I've set out to do enough random and unusual things in my life that Bryn is no longer surprised by my next idea, nor is she doubtful that I'll figure out how to get it done.

This book was a bit different, though. Whereas things like

beer and sailboats are what I'd consider my "neat to do" projects, this book fell into a different category. This was a "need to do." It also didn't fall into the class of "I don't know about this, but I want to learn" endeavors. I had spent many years of my life working with procurement and supply chain teams. I knew that working in those areas felt like constantly running around like my hair was on fire. Somehow "hair on fire" had become the norm in most supply chain environments. With the burning happening so frequently, it's possible to become desensitized to the smoke of new risks ahead. It's time we talked about the fire while also providing solutions to douse the flames. Sourcing does not have to be so difficult.

When I think about sourcing, the role of finding the right parts in the right places at the right time and in the right quantity, today, I think of an old picture my mom used to have hanging in her kitchen. It said, "Housework is something you do that nobody notices unless you don't do it." Supply chain management (the sourcing piece in particular) is exactly like that. When things are going smoothly, rarely are the leaders of a company celebrating the supply chain employees for bringing ease to the company's existence. When supply chain associates are doing things right, nobody notices.

COVID-19 gave people around the world a first-hand experience of what happens when supply chains are disrupted. That was probably the first time in most Americans' lives when they worried about having enough toilet paper. It was also the first time my teenage daughter and mother seemed even remotely interested in the work I did, wanting to understand why they could no longer get what they wanted when they wanted it. The COVID era was more than just a "hair on fire" moment for supply chain professionals. We were facing issues that more closely resembled the two-story bonfires at Burning Man events. Supply chain teams, especially those in sourcing, work so incredibly hard to keep business and life moving along smoothly. It's time that they get more positive attention and real solutions to the challenges they are constantly looking to solve.

But Bryn brought up a very solid point, as she usually does. How was I going to create a book about the current and emerging issues with sourcing and data that didn't sound like the "wah-wah" droning voice of the teacher in the *Peanuts* cartoons or read like the world's longest sales brochure? I committed myself to the goal: write a book on the importance of contextualized data and do it in a way that honors the reader's time and provides real, actionable insights and tools. Oh, and make it fun.

THE BOOK IS MIGHTIER THAN THE SLIDE DECK

Presentations can be great. I've given my fair share of presentations on the tremendous amount of data that today's supply chain teams are faced with—something I refer to as the Data Gulch. I've talked plenty about how this Data Gulch results in the formation of a Decision Abyss, making it more challenging for sourcing associates to make the best data-driven decisions. The challenge in using presentations as a form of information sharing is that there just isn't time to go deep enough into the core of the issue and solve it. It's like trying to show people what's in the Mariana Trench, the deepest oceanic point, and handing everyone scuba gear to do it. You can't get down far enough to know what you're really facing.

Aside from that, I have always had a love of books and have been an avid reader for most of my life. In fact, back in my college years and long before we had Amazon reviews to guide us in our book selections, I had my own book review website where I would offer my thoughts on which books were worth reading and which ones, in my not-so-humble opinion, could collect dust. One thing I've admired about nearly all books, though, is that they seem to have the same goal: to make life better for the reader. Some books set out to do that through entertainment, while others provide research or life hacks to optimize health or athletic performance. Books may challenge our way of thinking, help us develop new neural pathways, and compel us to expand or change our viewpoints.

I value your time and your precious resource of mental energy. This book will illuminate new ways of working so that your mental energy will no longer have to be expended on the tedium of trying to discover the best source of truth in your purchasing decisions. For business leaders who walk around with the invisible weight of managing risk on their shoulders, I hope that you finish this book with a new and enlightened perspective on what sourcing risks actually are and how they can be mitigated.

I needed to share my knowledge on improving the work of people in sourcing and procurement and the quality of decision making in companies with supply chain teams. It needed to be in a book format because these concepts take time to digest, and you may need to revisit them. This book is the starting point of the conversations that we cannot afford to avoid any longer. Thanks to increased globalization, geopolitical tensions, and the rapid evolution of technology, we've reached a tipping point in sourcing. Those who know how to make sense of (or contextualize) all their data will survive while the rest will perpetually struggle to keep up. It's time to tell a new story in which the corporate Goliath or the big bully with the deepest pockets doesn't automatically win. We're going on the hero's journey: product sourcing edition!

HOW DID WE GET HERE AND WHERE ARE WE GOING?

Maybe you've read this far and you're not sure if this applies to you. Or perhaps you know it applies to you, but suddenly you are feeling reluctant to face the issue of current data overwhelm and the antiquated approach to data-driven decision making that most companies are still using. In this book, I'll be discussing the *what* of the current Data Gulch that has been created by decades of data proliferation, and how this Data Gulch results in what I call a Decision Abyss for making strategic sourcing choices.

The phenomenon of the Decision Abyss exists at every company that makes products. While it's most evident in manufacturing companies, retail companies that are trying to stock the right products at the right levels also face data-driven decision-making challenges due to this Decision Abyss. For the sake of this book, however, I want to zero in on manufacturing companies. Even more specifically, I want to speak to the direct material sourcing piece of procurement. If that sounds like you or a component of the business you're a part of, you're in the right place!

Once you understand what got us to this state of data overwhelm, I'll discuss how we can use this data to identify what market risks really are and then work to reduce them. I'll also discuss how we often have more buying options than we realize and can use contextualized data to make better buying decisions that will save us money. The icing on this data cake is that we can do these things while simplifying the role of supply chain experts.

At this point in most presentations, I usually get one of three responses:

1. "This sounds a bit too good to be true!"

2. "There is no way my company will invest in this. We rarely get funding for new supply chain technology!"

3. "You will have to pry these Excel spreadsheets and Outlook emails from my cold, dead hands, Keith!"

It certainly won't come to that. There's no need to get your "Coupa is life" tattoo permanently removed from your body either. My goal is not to force you to change. What want is for you to take a critical look at why you or the people you work with may be resistant to changing how things are done. We'll swim through the history and evolution of the supply chain and procurement sector. We'll dive into reasons why what is right for sourcing may be at odds with what is right for your business as a whole. Perhaps most importantly, we'll take the plunge into analyzing human behavior and what drives our resistance to change—how we're wired to favor safety or risk aversion over making a change that could have a tremendous gain. And we'll do it all with a healthy dose of water metaphors and storytelling, because water is the essence of life and the backbone of the global economy, with approximately 90 percent of international trade traveling by sea.

Stay hydrated, readers. We've got quite the journey ahead!

SECTION 1

LOST
AT SEA

ONE

WHEN THE WAVE HITS

It almost always starts with a wave. Sometimes it's an actual wave, like the 2011 Tohoku earthquake and tsunami in Japan that devastated ports and factories, causing production halts for companies like Toyota and Nissan. More often, though, it's a metaphorical wave that rocks the supply chain and sends a company's sourcing team into a frenzy.

An often-overlooked department, sourcing now finds all company eyes (and expectations) on them. The pressure on sourcing teams is intense. They need to figure out where and how to procure new parts, metals, ingredients, and materials to keep production moving. Meanwhile, customers are getting frustrated by not being able to have what they want when they want it. The finance department wants to know, "How much is this going to cost us?" The engineers don't want to go back and redesign or look for alternative parts. The sales team is freaking out about getting products to market so they meet their key performance indicators (KPIs). The admin team is stocking extra bagels and coffee in the breakroom—whatever will motivate sourcing to solve the problem quickly. On top of that, Bob, who has worked for the company's sourcing team for over twenty years says, "Hold my spreadsheet!" and opts for early retirement rather than going through another round of *this* again.

Somehow sourcing does it. They almost always seem to figure it out, even if it means using several butterfly bandages to try and close a wound that really calls for stitches. They make the best decisions they can with the tools they have and hope they'll have a semi-decent reprieve until the next supply chain shockwave hits. Sometimes, when they get too exhausted from repeating this cycle, they find me and my company, LevaData.

The shocks our customers experience vary by industry and geography. If I asked one hundred people today for an example of a supply chain disruption, most would likely still point to COVID-19. It was a massive supply chain shock that impacted nearly all industries. The electronics supply chain alone found that their lead times were five times longer than usual. However, there are multitudes of other supply chain shocks our clients experience that are more regional or specific. Each one causes a panic of some degree. Some are resolved more quickly than others.

Supply chain shocks may be related to natural disasters, like the Japanese tsunami I mentioned earlier, or the Texas freeze of 2022 that caused widespread power outages and shut down several semiconductor plants. A supply chain may experience a shock due to war, such as when Russia invaded Ukraine in February of 2022, resulting in the largest and deadliest war in Europe since World War II. The invasion shined a light on many of the raw materials and natural resources that Ukraine provides. It's the supplier of approximately 50 percent of the world's neon gas, an important raw material used by the semiconductor industry. The country also holds significant reserves of resources like uranium, graphite, titanium, and lithium, which are crucial materials for industries ranging from electronics and energy to defense and manufacturing. It forced Boeing to diversify its supply base rapidly, leading to sourcing delays and pressure on aircraft delivery schedules.

There are macroeconomic factors that can disrupt a supply chain like inflation and tariffs. At the time of writing this book, the US's uncertain but potentially massive tariff policy is sending sourcing teams into a frenzy as they try to determine where to get materials from without having too significant of an impact on their cost of goods sold. Geopolitical relations can shake up a supply chain as well. With each change in elected leadership, tensions and sanctions shift, favoring some countries over others.

In so many of these cases, companies did not look at changing their supply chain processes until the moment they were forced to. They may not have diversified geographically or researched alternate suppliers for their most essential product components. They did know how to identify alternate part numbers to find what they needed if a supplier's inventory ran out. There wasn't necessarily the time to create a backup plan. There wasn't the energy to really identify and mitigate risks. Instead, they waited for the inevitable shockwave to hit and *then* took action. But why?

Before I risk potentially inducing PTSD symptoms in any readers who have or do work in sourcing, I want to take a moment to get clear on terminology. To really understand what we're dealing with here, we all must speak the same language. I've met plenty of folks who use terms like "procurement" interchangeably with "sourcing." Others use "procurement" interchangeably with "supply chain" to describe their departments. To me, it's like trying to use "putt-putt" and "golf" interchangeably—there are similarities, but if you try to drive off the tee at a putt-putt, you will be escorted out by security. The two games are not the same.

A supply chain is a network of activities, organizations, resources, and technologies involved in the production and delivery of a product or service from the initial supplier to the final customer. It encompasses every stage of the process, including direct material sourcing of all parts, metals, and ingredients for production, manufacturing, transportation and logistics, warehousing, distribution, and retail or end customers. The goal of a supply chain is to ensure the efficient, cost-effective, and timely delivery of goods and services while meeting customer demand and maintaining quality.

Procurement is a subset of the supply chain ecosystem specifically focused on the process of acquiring goods and services. Historically procurement has been defined by software vendors and consultants as having two key workflows: Source-to-Contract (S2C) and Procure-to-Pay (P2P). When you merge these two key workflows, you get the overarching procurement workflow known as Source-to-Pay (S2P), encompassing the entire process of sourcing goods, negotiating contracts, receiving goods, and making payments.

Sourcing is the most important aspect of the procurement workflow, where you can gain a disproportionate return on investment (ROI). It is identifying and evaluating the suppliers who provide the pieces or raw materials you need. This book is specifically focused on the sourcing function of manufacturing companies, the current risks affecting them, and how they can evolve their processes to succeed in the coming era. I geek out on sourcing because I know that for the companies who value it, it is the thing that becomes a real competitive advantage.

Sourcing is one of the most valuable activities within a complete supply chain workflow. It often has the most data variables and can be the biggest driver of both product cost and profitability. This value is determined by the number of parts that need to be sourced, the number of alternative options available for those parts, and the diversity and distance in where those parts are sourced from. The supply chain shock a company might experience is heavily impacted by their available options and how they may or may not have alternative suppliers, options for purchasing, and the ability to make a change.

What I've found with most companies we work with at LevaData is that if they get sourcing right, then everything else in the supply chain becomes an easier problem to solve and they can give their company a strategic advantage in the market, sometimes over much larger or well-established competitors. When it comes to the supply of parts, metals, ingredients, or materials, having the knowledge of your options and having the agility to change to those options is a game-changer. *He who hath the parts gets the customer.* In fact, if we're looking at the value in the whole procurement workflow, I would estimate you can find at least 80 percent of the value specifically within the sourcing function. It's not only the *what* and *at what cost*; it's receiving it at the right time for production so that everything continues to run efficiently.

For example, if one or two of those components is missing or unavailable in a technology product that takes one hundred individual components to make, you no longer have a product to sell. It doesn't matter that sourcing got the other ninety-eight parts at a great price and at the right time. It doesn't matter if you have a great design team, a great sales team, or an accounts receivable clerk who stays on top of customer payments. Sourcing drives the cost of the product. Sourcing drives the availability of the product. So why don't companies invest more in sourcing?

My hunch is that most companies feel like they do invest in sourcing. While sourcing may not get the big budget, many sourcing teams I've met with have no shortage of technology programs, software, apps, or coworkers collaborating in pursuit of their goals. They have tools to get the job done, though not necessarily the right tools or the best tools. The industry has been like this for so long that sourcing teams have learned to normalize pain to the point that they may not even realize how much pain they're in. Why? Because they've never had the opportunity to experience anything different.

It reminds me of the time I was building an addition on

my house. I'm certainly no seasoned construction worker, but I love to learn and am pretty good at problem solving. There I was, with my hammer and a bucket of nails, building away and enjoying the slow but steady progress I was making. At first it was fun, even satisfying, to feel the swing of the hammer and the way it could drive a sinker nail into the wood. Sure, I felt some pain, but I figured I was supposed to. The pain is how I measured that I was working hard. Unfortunately, it took fewer nails than I would like to admit for my shoulder to be sore and my arm muscles to begin fatiguing. The frame wasn't even a tenth of the way up and I was becoming less enchanted by my "pain equals productivity" mentality. This was going to be exhausting.

My father-in-law, who knows a thing or two about construction, came over and gave a quick laugh.

"What are you using a hammer for?" he asked before walking back to his car and pulling out a nail gun.

Now listen: it's not that I didn't know that nail guns existed. Of course nail guns were an option on the market for people who wanted to drive nails into wood. But for some reason I felt like I didn't need the extra expensive equipment. After all, part of the reason for me building the addition myself was to save money. Why would I spend more on a tool when my trusty hammer would probably be fine? My father-in-law raised an eyebrow and handed me the new tool. All it took was one shot from the nail gun and I was a convert. It was so easy. It felt effortless compared to my hammer. On top of that, the quality of the output was better. The nails went in quickly and straight. The physical pain of using the nail gun was almost nothing compared to my previous tool. Why had I not opened myself up to trying a different way earlier?

Lessons often take time (and repeated pain) for us to really internalize them. I learned this lesson again when I started my hobby of hand-shaping surfboards. When it comes to surfboards, balance is key. The thickness of the board must be consistent and accurate to provide the correct amount of float for the weight of the surfer. If the board is too thin, there will be less flotation. This makes paddling difficult and it is harder to balance if you do catch a wave. If the board is too thick, it becomes harder to maneuver and makes duck-diving in big waves far more challenging.

When I started hand-shaping surfboards, I relied on the precision of my measuring tape and my eyesight to measure the board's thickness. It was fine. It was simple and it worked, so I kept doing it and getting decent results. But, in the process I could have been crafting boards that were better. I just didn't think to look into alternative tools for a while because I could manage with what I had.

At some point, though, I became the proud owner of a caliper, a precision measuring tool used to gauge the thickness, width, diameter, or depth of an object. This upgraded tool turned out to be an absolute game changer in the way I worked and in the quality of what I produced. Not only did it make measuring far easier, but my results improved dramatically because I was working with more accurate data.

The lesson in both these stories is that we can have impactful results when we use the right tool for the right job. These experiences didn't cause me to toss my hammer or tape measure in the trash. Hammers are great for small jobs around the house, like hanging a picture frame. And my tape measurer was incredibly handy in determining if the chair my daughter ordered off the internet could actually fit through the doorway of her bedroom. But I would never go back to using a hammer on another major construction project and will never produce a surfboard without a caliper again. Once you discover a means to accomplish things in an easier way, it's nearly impossible to go back to the old way of working. *Use the right tool for the right job.*

This same lesson can be applied to sourcing technology. When it comes to the sourcing profession, many companies are working with outdated, almost obsolete technology. I'm both surprised and not at all surprised when I encounter a company relying on spreadsheets and emails to manage their suppliers and parts pricing. Spreadsheets and emails seem to dominate the sourcing landscape.

The challenge with spreadsheets and emails is that they create mostly manual processes which require the direct input of sourcing professionals to update and share data. Things can become even more challenging for sourcing teams when Joanne, who has become a silo of knowledge in her specific slice of sourcing, decides to quit her job and move to an ashram in the Bahamas. The rest of the team is left scrambling, trying to make sense of her files and figure out what knowledge or relationships may have been lost in the transition.

Many organizations not only rely on outdated technology

but also use the wrong tools for sourcing and procurement. While the market offers numerous supply chain management platforms packed with features, these solutions often prioritize breadth over depth. They can do a little bit for many areas of the supply chain, benefitting a greater number of people at the company, but not to the level of support that they truly need. The sourcing piece of the supply chain operates in a data-rich environment that demands complex and specialized capabilities that can manage many inputs and provide clear, contextualized outputs. Using a generic supply chain system for sourcing is like boarding a cruise ship to explore the Mariana Trench—initially appealing with its many features, but ultimately ineffective for the deep, complex work required. To achieve true efficiency and insight, organizations need technology built purposefully for sourcing and procurement.

How did we end up in this position with sourcing teams not having the right tools for their work? I've found there are two primary drivers that keep sourcing in the technological dark: 1) sourcing is often one of the last groups to be taken care of within a company; and 2) there can be an "it's just the way we do things" mentality within sourcing. In my experience, sourcing departments are often underfunded and overutilized.

Sourcing professionals are evaluated on metrics like cost avoidance and purchase order cycle time. When they make purchasing decisions or negotiate contracts to meet these KPIs, they typically accomplish these results due to their own manual efforts and negotiating savvy. I've met many sourcing professionals and teams who are quite talented at meeting their KPIs quarter after quarter, year after year. Ironically, it's because they *can* accomplish their goals and continue to do so that they are rarely given the funding to invest in tools that make their jobs easier. In a data-heavy job, they are not given the tools that support data-driven decision making.

Additionally, sourcing professionals don't always demand the tools. Sometimes they aren't even aware of the tools available to them (like me with the surfboard caliper). They default to their usual program because it's how they've always done things, and it works. They're sticking with the old measuring tape and hoping for the best. It's a method that works for them...until it doesn't.

We are approaching a real flexion point in supply chain management where we can no longer fall back on how things have always been done. Global competition, the evolution of technology, increasing depth of data, and our own mental health won't allow things to remain the same. I understand why sourcing professionals are reluctant to change. They are already taxed for time. Who would want to sign up to learn a new program when your days are maxed out? They're also under-resourced. The many programs they do have often overburden them with processes and information that don't quite get them what they need. "Tedious" is a word I hear often.

Since about the 1990s, the amount of data that sourcing teams must work with has grown exponentially. The increase in data has three main drivers. First, the growth of a globally competitive market allows us to source from more places than ever before. Second, the rapid evolution of technology and AI is creating new data at an almost unimaginable pace. Technology's evolving data storage solutions allow the storage and manipulation of data like never before. Lastly, thanks to companies like Amazon, consumer tastes have changed. Buyers are able to price compare online and the acceptable wait time to receive products has been reduced to almost nothing.

For a process like sourcing, which is still largely human-powered, we are running out of bandwidth to do what technology can do when it comes to making sense of data. We could stare at a spreadsheet or search the internet for hours and discover the hundreds of global suppliers that make a certain part, then we could try to decide which one is the right one for us to go with based on price, geography, lead times, and their ability to meet demand. We make the best data-driven decision we can in hours, days, or weeks when there is technology that can do it in a fraction of the time.

In the next few chapters, I'll explain more about the history and modern context of how we've arrived here in the supply chain, and sourcing specifically. For now, though, there is one key component of sourcing today that we need to address. It's what I call the Decision Abyss and I believe it's going to be one of the defining factors in how manufacturing companies fare over the next several years.

Some might view too much data as a good problem to have. It means we have no shortage of options. There are actually people in this world who love the book-sized menu of The Cheesecake Factory or the fact that you can go to your local grocery store and choose from over twenty varieties of plain tortilla chips. Sourcing individuals, however, could potentially drown in the amount of data available to them while trying to make their decisions. Their companies may have been tracking and housing data on parts, pricing, and customer buying habits for decades. Internet search engines and marketplaces have companies entering and exiting the supplier arena daily. What we are left with is the Decision Abyss.

The Decision Abyss is a term that I use to describe what's going on at companies between three different functions: between engineering and product design, between supply chain and all things supply chain planning, and in procurement (specifically sourcing). And this Decision Abyss is preventing companies from making better-informed decisions. The Abyss happens because each of these respected functions has tools, processes, and germane knowledge that's developed over time by which they run their own business. It's like trying to coordinate peace talks between countries without having a common language through which to communicate and negotiate. Sourcing is a highly manual process that is driven by people. What results is various teams not communicating effectively inside the company.

While the Decision Abyss phenomenon can develop across many industries, it most often exists in manufacturing. Sourcing professionals need data from enterprise resource planning (ERP), procurement, product design, and engineering. Unfortunately, this data from each department can become siloed and is held captive in a variety of enterprise systems, ranging from spreadsheets and emails to data lakes, data swamps, and other shared data stores and structures. The amount of data and the fact that it is housed in disparate siloes hinders business workflow, decision making, and how people collaborate.

Sourcing ends up in the center of this whirlpool of competing needs. The ERP houses information on parts data, inventory, and payments. The supply chain organization is sharing how sourcing's work is going to impact warehousing, transportation, and labor management. The product design and engineering teams want sourcing to account for the product lifecycle management and ever-changing bill of materials (BOM). Procurement is trying to manage contract life cycles, supplier risk, and accounts payable, among many other things. You can see how the Abyss starts to form.

The Decision Abyss is derived from a lack of easy-to-understand data that drives informed and cross-functional decision making. It is the result of failure to aggregate and contextualize data and produces asymmetric information, which leads to decision making without having the complete picture. It creates defensive or reactive supply chain decisions.

While the Decision Abyss is where bad decisions are made, it's not the root of the problem. It's a symptom of something much deeper. It's the tip of the metaphorical iceberg that you can see, which is why companies continue to invest in systems that are supposed to help teams and departments collaborate and share information more effectively. What they don't see is the tremendous amount of data lurking below the surface. What makes the underlying data so dangerous is that it is often stored in different pockets or divisions of a company. All that data is missing important context related to other data pieces and they often lack a single source of truth that validates the data's accuracy. The result of this is what I call the Data Gulch. It's the state of company data that makes it nearly impossible to use for intelligent, data-driven decision making.

My daughter inadvertently created a pretty good visual of the Decision Abyss concept when she was a toddler. In a very short period of time, and in the way that only toddlers seem to have the powers to be able to do, she found our collection of jigsaw puzzles and dumped every single one onto the floor in a big pile. She could have made snow angels in the puzzle pieces, there were so many. Now imagine if I had invited some friends over and said, "Hey everyone, you each have a puzzle to put together. Start digging!" Chances are nobody would be very successful, and Bryn and I would likely not have been invited to future social gatherings. But if we had a way to sort the pieces first, determine if this red piece belonged with this box or that box, we would be able to provide everyone with material they could actually work with.

If companies want to make better decisions—ones that could result in cost savings, partial visibility inside of the BOM, and improved finished goods predictability—they need data points that are contextualized. What that means is mapping the data we have so that it all makes sense. Contextualized data means working down to the parts or raw material level and translating it into the same "language" that can be used by engineering, across the supply chain, and specifically by sourcing. Contextualizing data means creating a framework for it to make sense so that people know what they're working with.

To know where we're headed, we must understand where we came from and how we got here in the first place. Studying our history should illuminate why what we've always done has worked for us over the past few decades. It will also show you why we can no longer afford to proceed in this same way. Like Kodak or Blockbuster Video, it does not serve us to dig our heels in and ignore the inevitable change required to remain competitive. It's time to take a real look at where we're coming from and where we're heading. Put your dive gear on. It's time to explore!

TWO

FROM RIPPLES TO WAVES:
The Ever-Changing Currents of Supply Chains

One of my favorite stories that I find myself referring to often is the Taoist parable of the farmer and his neighbor. I was first introduced to it in a book I highly recommend called *Positive Intelligence* by Shirzad Chamine. There are many of variations of the Taoist story. Here's one of them:

> A Chinese farmer lived in the countryside with his son and a beautiful horse that they loved and cared for. One day the farmer decided to enter his horse into a village contest. When he won the contest and some prize money, the farmer's neighbor said, "Oh, what luck to have such a remarkable horse. Congratulations!" To the neighbor's surprise, the farmer simply shrugged his shoulders and said, "Who knows what's good or bad?"
>
> Some days later, thieves learned of the prize-winning horse and stole it in the middle of the night. The neighbor returned to share his condolences at the farmer's tremendous loss. The farmer astonished the neighbor once again when he responded with a shrug, saying, "Who knows what's good or bad?"

CONQUERING THE DECISION ABYSS

A week or so later, the horse escaped from the thieves, returning to his beloved farmer. Several other wild horses returned to the farm with him. The neighbor was in shock. "What incredibly good fortune you have!" he said, to which the farmer gave his signature reaction: a shrug and the phrase, "Who knows what's good or bad?"

As the farmer's son was working to tame one of the new, spirited horses, he was thrown off and badly broke his leg. "Oh, how terrible!" the neighbor replied as he came over to show compassion to the family. The farmer shrugged and said, "Who knows what's good or bad?"

A short time later, the royal army passed through town to recruit all able-bodied young men to fight in a war. The farmer's son was passed over due to his shattered leg. This time, as the neighbor stopped over to share a meal with the farmer and his son, he knew not to comment with any sort of emotional judgment about the positive or negative nature of the situation. He was pretty sure he knew how the farmer would respond.

The point of this parable is that while we may be quick to assign a feeling or label of "good" or "bad" to things in life, we often lack the full context and foresight to really know. The Taoist philosophy illustrated in this story is that good and bad are almost always interwoven and inseparable. It reminds us that when we make judgments based on our initial feelings of good or bad, we may mislead ourselves.

What does that have to do with the history of the supply chain? As I see it, with each iteration of supply chain evolution, with each turn of the wheel, we can see how things can be both good and bad. Every innovation creates winners and losers. With each modernization, some problems are eliminated, and some new problems are created. There is no single event that we may be able to characterize as "all good" or "all bad" (except for maybe when the Coca-Cola company released what became unofficially known as "New Coke" in 1985—that was really bad).

I've found that within supply chain management, and specifically sourcing, there are people who can slip into this mentality of "good" and "bad" with their work. I see this most often when people are faced with a problem that feels so unique, so unusual, that the solutions appear nearly impossible to come by. They may feel that the amount of data available to them is completely overwhelming, unorganized, or unusable. To use my favorite description of the problem: the data is not contextualized or blended together to empower cross-data insights and action.

I remember a conversation I had with a young sourcing professional who expressed his frustration at needing to source one specific part that he claimed only came from one specific supplier. He felt he was at the mercy of whatever the supplier demanded because there were no other options. In his mind, this left zero room for negotiation, which was especially frustrating since he was evaluated annually based on the cost savings he had achieved. The situation left him feeling disempowered. Fortunately, I was able to share with him the power of contextualized data and the world of alternate, equivalent parts (more on them in Chapter 7). He would take this lesson forward for the rest of his sourcing career. Solutions did exist. He simply didn't know how to find them.

While every manufacturer may face unique circumstances or have unique products, the supply chain challenges they face are often similar. One common issue is that there are constant direct material sourcing challenges. This creates spend complexity based on what the manufacturing company says materials need to cost for the product to be profitable compared to the prices that the materials market sets.

Limited supply resources are another huge barrier for manufacturers. It is something that is becoming more evident as everything from cars to toaster ovens to cars-that-look-like-toaster-ovens have increased in technological complexity. Many products have become more like minicomputers, which has created increased competition for semiconductors worldwide. During COVID, when semiconductors were extremely limited, some companies went back to the drawing board to redesign their products rather than try to compete for limited supply. We saw companies like Audi that went so far as to release cars with a "Semiconductor Shortage" package that dropped the price of the vehicle by hundreds to thousands of dollars but took away features like blind spot monitoring, rear collision detection, and wireless charging pads.

External factors like market volatility present a constant threat, yet they're not unexpected threats. We expect market pricing and availability to be in some state of constant movement, though some markets move far more than others. The challenge that my new sourcing friend experienced was one of limited and fragmented data that created a barrier to identifying more possible solutions.

One final challenge that many manufacturing companies face is that upper management can be slow to make decisions. When trying to navigate the speed of market volatility and production demand in a company with a slow decision-making process, it may feel virtually impossible to plan accordingly. For example, a mid-sized electronics manufacturer faced significant delays in approving critical supply chain adjustments. When a key component suddenly became scarce, the procurement team identified an equivalent part that could keep production on schedule. However, upper management took weeks to approve the switch due to lengthy internal reviews. By the time they reached a decision, the alternative part had also become unavailable, forcing the company to halt production and miss key delivery deadlines, resulting in lost revenue and strained customer relationships.

In dealing with these similar challenges, most manufacturing companies also face similar consequences. The first issue created is that companies are leaving money on the table when they could be buying better, smarter, or more efficiently. They often do not realize how much money they're losing because they lack contextualized data to even understand what their alternate options are. That lack of knowledge exposes companies to greater market risk because they are limited in their decision making. As a result, companies' products are less profitable than they could be.

In the past, I loved to illustrate these sourcing challenges and risks in some of my presentations by using the iPhone as an example. I would speak about the complexity and challenges for a company like Apple to source the 600 individual components (now it's fewer than that) that make up one phone.

"Imagine what a monumental task it is to manage the cost, inventory, and timing of each of those parts so that production can meet customer demands on time and in the right quantities!" I would say.

The attendees' heads would nod in agreement that this was a real challenge that Apple must have a heck of a time managing all those spreadsheets and emails. How could they possibly manage the complexity with the tools that today's modern sourcing professionals use?

And then one day I learned the truth: Apple isn't using the same tools as most sourcing professionals. I had an Apple employee in my audience who shared that they have built their own sophisticated in-house technology to reduce or eliminate the complexity that so many other companies face. Of course they did. Of course they designed tools to sift through the incredible amount of data available to them to make the most agile, cost-effective sourcing decisions. They're Apple, regularly holding the #1 spot worldwide in market capitalization. They have the technical know-how and the financial resources to identify these very real sourcing problems and solve them without waiting on the market to design something to meet their needs. Nearly every other manufacturing company worldwide is without this strategic advantage.

Why share this story? It highlights three things: 1) these sourcing challenges are very real and need to be addressed;

2) most manufacturing companies do not have the resources to solve these sourcing challenges; and 3) there are Apple and other manufacturing giants that small- and medium-sized manufacturing companies need to figure out how to compete with. The resource and knowledge gap are widening between companies, increasing the barriers to entry and creating challenges for existing companies. If you're not a major player in today's market, it may feel like you've been hung out to dry. But as the Taoist parable advised us, we can't always know if something is truly good or bad.

I believe that to thoroughly understand our current sourcing situation, we need to understand where we came from and how we got here in the first place. If we were doctors trying to make a medical diagnosis, we would start with the patient's health history. For context on the current issues impacting supply chain management, and specifically sourcing, we need to understand the historical context that got us to this point.

PRE-INDUSTRIAL AND EARLY INDUSTRIAL ERA

The concept of managing supply chains is as old as trade itself. In the pre-industrial era, supply chain management was manual and localized. Merchants relied on ledgers and verbal agreements to track inventory and manage trade routes. These were the days of customers buying two bags of flour and the merchants having them sign a book or ledger to track the transaction.

With the rise of industrialization in the nineteenth century, businesses began facing greater complexity, necessitating more systematic approaches to track production, inventory, and distribution. In the early twentieth century, basic forms of automation emerged. Pioneering companies used punch cards and early mechanical computing devices to manage inventory and order processing. However, these systems were rigid, costly, and only accessible to the largest corporations.

MID-TWENTIETH CENTURY:
The Birth of Computing and Early Supply Chain Systems

In 1956, Malcolm McLean invented the standardized shipping container. This relatively simple creation revolutionized cargo shipments, significantly impacting the way that goods were shipped across long distances. This new standardization meant increased efficiency in loading times at ports and reduced shipping costs by around 25 percent, spurring an increase in companies' abilities to trade globally.

In the same era, we witnessed the advent of computing, which brought new possibilities for managing supply chains. Early enterprise software was developed to address specific needs in manufacturing and logistics. For example, material requirements planning (MRP) systems emerged in the 1960s to assist manufacturers in planning production schedules and inventory requirements once more material options became available to them. It helped companies to better manage what they could produce based on the inventory they had on hand and allowed them to more easily identify what materials they would need to produce their lava lamps or Braun T3 radio transmitters. The MRP systems used basic algorithms to calculate the materials needed for production based on demand forecasts, BOMs, and inventory levels. This marked the beginning of digitized supply chain management. However, these systems were still limited in scope, focusing primarily on production efficiency rather than end-to-end supply chain visibility.

1970s–1980s: *Integration and Expansion*

The 1970s saw the rise of ERP systems, which expanded on MRP by integrating additional business functions, such as accounting, procurement, and human resources. ERP systems provided a unified view of operations, making it easier for companies to manage their supply chains holistically.

During this time, companies like SAP and Oracle began developing modular software solutions that could be tailored to specific business needs. They were two of the largest enterprise software companies on the planet. Complex data constructs began. In parallel, advancements in computing power and database management made it possible to handle more complex datasets, laying the groundwork for modern supply chain software.

In the 1980s, the concept of *manufacturing* resource planning (MRP II) emerged, building on MRP to include capacity planning, shop-floor control, and demand forecasting. This marked a shift toward more sophisticated supply chain management, emphasizing collaboration and data-driven decision making. This was the start of large and difficult data sets that still impact us today. It's where the Taoist parable really starts to come into play. Was this shift for the general betterment of supply chain management or the beginning of a challenging road ahead?

1990s: *The Globalization Era*

Remember the dawn of the internet on your home computer? The ear-splitting dial-up sound that seemed to define the decade? The 1990s were transformative for supply chain software due to the twin forces of the internet and globalization. As businesses expanded internationally, supply chains became more complex and interdependent. Businesses couldn't operate in a vacuum anymore. Suddenly we all had more transparency into how other manufacturers were operating.

In this decade traditional systems were no longer sufficient to manage the intricacies of global trade, leading to the development of more advanced tools. Supply chain management (SCM) software emerged as a distinct category, focusing on optimizing the entire supply chain, from sourcing to delivery. Companies like i2 Technologies, Manugistics, and JD Edwards introduced solutions for demand planning, logistics optimization, and supplier management.

The rise of the internet also enabled the development of web-based supply chain solutions, facilitating real-time communication and collaboration between supply chain part-ners. This period saw the introduction of electronic data inter-change (EDI) standards, which allowed businesses to share critical information, such as purchase orders and shipping notifications, electronically. IBM was a huge provider of EDI solutions and really drove widespread market adoption.

For me, this period started to feel like the Wild West. You had older companies who continued to function using older, legacy systems. Then you had other companies working to evolve their technology, along with new companies who were doing things that the world had never seen before. The gap continued to widen in how companies managed their supply chain and sourcing functions—some clung to traditional meth-ods and some fully embraced the newest technologies available, even if they weren't perfect, to figure out what it could mean for their data storage and decision making.

2000s: *The Era of Automation and Analytics*

The early 2000s marked a shift toward automation and data analytics in supply chain management. It was the era of new and specialized tools. Advances in computing power, coupled with the proliferation of data, enabled companies to adopt more sophisticated programs for forecasting, optimization, and risk management.

The early 2000s were marked by the development of sev-eral key systems:

1. Advanced Planning and Scheduling (APS): These
    tools offered enhanced capabilities for production
    planning and distribution optimization, helping
    businesses align supply with demand more effectively.
2. Warehouse Management Systems (WMS): Software
    like Manhattan Associates and Blue Yonder intro-
    duced sophisticated tools for inventory tracking,
    order fulfillment, and warehouse optimization.
3. Transportation Management Systems (TMS): Tools
    for managing freight, optimizing routes, and reduc-
    ing transportation costs gained popularity.
4. Customer Relationship Management (CRM)
    Integration: SCM software began integrating with
    CRM systems to provide a seamless flow of informa-
    tion from demand generation to order fulfillment.
5. Cloud Computing: The adoption of cloud-based
    solutions began to accelerate, offering greater scal-
    ability, lower upfront costs, and easier collaboration
    across geographies.

The shift to Cloud Computing suddenly atrophied the
large data systems of the '70s, '80s, and '90s. Companies no
longer needed enormous warehouses to store their data. There
came the laborious task of transitioning all that supply chain
data from the old systems into the cloud and determining what
mattered, what didn't matter, and how it should all be organized. Many companies struggled with this transition and
ended up with large amounts of disparate data in their systems.

Cloud technology represents another intertwining of the benefits and challenges that can arise from change.

In this new era of automation, procurement was losing the fight in getting the attention (and budgets) from their CEOs and CFOs. While the tools were available, company budgets were instead allocated toward software tools for the marketing department, ERPs for the finance department, and complex CRMs for the sales teams. During this time, I worked for a supply chain software company, and I vividly remember one of our largest clients, a major name in computer manufacturing at that time, showing us their procurement management tools that were sixteen years old! While sixteen isn't old when it comes to tortoises or redwood trees, it felt ancient in the ever-evolving world of software. But the procurement team somehow did their job with what they had, so they didn't receive sufficient funding for upgrades.

2010s: *Digitization and the Rise of AI*

The 2010s were characterized by the digital transformation of supply chains. Companies began adopting technologies like artificial intelligence (AI), technology to simulate human learning, decision making, and problem solving. Machine learning (ML) was developed to take things a step further using algorithms and statistics for the computers to learn without specific instructions. This was also the dawn of the Internet of Things (IoT), multiple devices with the technology to connect, collect, and exchange data with each other. Today's smart homes, with security systems, video cameras, and doorbells that can be managed remotely from a smart phone, is one example.

All three of these developments helped to enhance supply chain visibility and responsiveness. AI and ML technologies enabled predictive analytics, allowing businesses to anticipate demand fluctuations, detect anomalies, and optimize inventory levels. IoT-connected devices, such as RFID tags and GPS trackers, provided real-time data on inventory, shipments, and equipment performance.

The 2010s also saw the introduction of blockchain technology in its nascent stages. Blockchain technology promised greater transparency and security in supply chain transactions, particularly for tracking goods and verifying authenticity. It was the era of cloud-native platforms, cloud-based supply chain management solutions that became the norm, offering real-time collaboration, faster deployment, and seamless integration with other business systems. This time was also marked by the explosive growth of e-commerce platforms like Amazon and Alibaba. Both companies pushed supply chain software to prioritize speed, agility, and customer satisfaction. They also had a tremendous impact on consumer expectations. We entered the area of ordering things and receiving them within a few days (or even a few hours) rather than a few weeks.

2020s AND BEYOND:
Toward Resilient and Sustainable Supply Chains

The COVID-19 pandemic underscored the importance of resilient and agile supply chains. Disruptions in global trade, labor shortages, and shifting consumer behaviors forced companies to re-evaluate their supply chain strategies. Companies became focused on greater resilience and risk management. Modern supply chain management software included tools for scenario planning, risk assessment, and real-time monitoring to help businesses respond to disruptions more effectively.

In 2019, Greta Thunberg was named *TIME Magazine*'s Person of the Year for her global climate change movement. In the COVID era, people were focused on sustainability and corporate social responsibility. Companies increasingly adopted supply chain software that could track carbon emissions, optimize resource usage, and support circular economy practices.

The 2020s became an area of hyperautomation. Supply chains were now integrating robotic process automation (RPA) with AI and ML into their processes. With the goal of increased efficiency, hyperautomation in supply chain operations served to reduce manual tasks in the supply chain process.

This period also saw a surge in the use of digital twin technologies, using virtual replicas of supply chain processes to allow businesses to simulate and optimize operations in real time. Digital twins date back to 2002 when Dr. Michael Grieves, then a faculty member of the University of Michigan, applied the digital twin concept to manufacturing. Perhaps one of my favorite examples of using digital twin technology in recent years comes from the award-winning Thames Water project. Nearly a quarter of the Thames Water network, which provides clean water to more than 15 million people, is lost due to insidious and invisible leaks in the system. Since creating a digital twin of the water network, Thames Water has been able to uncover a number of leaks caused by high pressure and damaged valves. It has allowed them to save a million liters of water every day!

INTO THE FUTURE

COVID was the most significant shockwave to supply chain management in the past several decades. While the COVID era might lead many supply chain professionals to say things like "that was a bad time," I might challenge them with a shrug. The COVID era shone a bright light on supply chain management. It was a major catalyst in the shift happening toward building more resilient, sustainable, and intelligent supply chains.

We're fortunate to live in these times when the supply chain is at the front of the conversation instead of at the back, where it's been historically. In the past, supply chain technology was leap-frogged by financial consolidation projects around ERP and other more emerging potentially more exciting technologies. Emerging technologies such as quantum computing, 5G, and advanced robotics are poised to further revolutionize the field, enabling businesses to navigate an increasingly interconnected and dynamic world. At the same time within the supply chain umbrella, procurement and specifically sourcing technologies continue to be overlooked and underfunded. Sourcing professionals still need to do their job effectively and efficiently for the respective companies they serve.

If you still feel like you're trying to get your feet under you from all the change that the COVID era brought, you're not alone. Many people are grasping to understand what exactly changed and where we are today in the world of supply chain management. Companies are seeking the best ways to optimize spending and build sourcing resilience for the future. With the expansion of AI-driven decision support, we are entering uncharted waters.

THREE

Staying Afloat
in Ever-Changing Conditions

My wife jokes that I often seem to have "supply chain on the brain." The other day we were walking through the mall and passed a discount shoe store. Those stores can be an outstanding place to shop if you happen to have a less common shoe size, like a women's 11 or men's 14, because you can often find popular styles available to you at a significantly reduced price. When I look at the overflowing selection of Nikes crafted for folks who I imagine are really good at sports like basketball, I wonder how many total units were overproduced. Here I am seeing evidence of overproduction at one store location. Imagine that extrapolated across North America or the world. Then my mind goes to the cost of overproduction and when companies miss their mark on their sales forecast. The cost of my popular-sized sneakers needs to go up to cover for the fact that there will be unsold inventory in other sizes. A poorly managed sourcing function costs both the company and the consumer money. A well-managed sourcing function can do just the opposite.

I hope this book grants more sourcing and procurement professionals permission to just say the thing. We need to talk about what is happening with sourcing today so that we can do something about it. Today's sourcing professionals have a lot to contend with. (Some would argue that it's too much to contend with.) There are the cumulative effects of historical factors to account for, like changes in technology and the digitization of products, plus the new wave tech evolution and even greater competition for resources at the best price possible.

Sourcing is in an era of increased stress and duress. Internally, sourcing professionals are facing new challenges with inventory management and pressure from other departments within their companies. Externally they are contending with geopolitical tension, growing competition for parts, metals, and ingredient materials, and the simultaneously risky and rewarding world of AI. Right before our eyes, the work of sourcing is changing. It's a time when agility is a necessity or you're at great risk of accidentally getting tossed overboard when the next wave hits.

In today's market I see four primary drivers of stress and duress amongst sourcing teams. The first is the constant need and pressure to reduce material costs and achieve savings (or cost-avoidance). Within nearly all companies, the supply chain or procurement departments are not revenue drivers that contribute to top-line growth for the company. They don't get the flashy sales meetings in Monaco where the top salespeople of the year are awarded lavish gifts on top of their already lavish bonuses. They don't get the kudos and back-slaps that the marketing team gets when they launch a new campaign that results in a healthy ROI. For sourcing teams to shine, they need to contribute to the company's bottom line with continual cost reduction. That is no small feat in today's era of inflation and increased competition.

One of the best ways a sourcing professional can meet or exceed their cost reduction goals is through having accurate and contextualized data on the suppliers who sell the materials they need and the most up-to-date pricing at their fingertips. Constant shifts in raw material costs and currency fluctuations make managing cost savings increasingly difficult. To make matters more challenging, many of today's procurement teams work with limited or lagging cost data depending on the age of their system. I've seen many market-leading companies still use spreadsheets to manage their vendors and price lists. They are trying to make the best decisions available with old or inaccurate data.

The second driver of stress and duress is the deep reliance on supplier relationships and collaboration. Sourcing professionals are participating in the delicate balance of negotiating the price they need, while maintaining a positive relationship with their suppliers. This becomes increasingly difficult when: 1) there is increased market competition for source material; and 2) the sourcing professional lacks (or is not aware of) other supplier options. Both factors reduce the sourcing professional's ability to impact pricing. Options equal negotiating power.

Not only are there new competitors entering the market, but there are new industries competing for materials that they've never needed before. Raw materials like lithium, cobalt, and copper have increased in demand over the past two decades due to the proliferation of high-tech products. Semiconductors, lithium-ion batteries, and specialized polymers are being used as components in more products than ever before. Sourcing professionals need to be aware of when new suppliers enter the market as potential resources while not losing sight of the competitive landscape for emerging industry players.

This brings us to the third driver of stress and duress: geopolitical tensions. Geography and country of origin now play a significant role in decision making. Geopolitical tensions may have an impact on currency fluctuations, which impact material prices. Everything from border closures, trade restrictions, tariffs, and trade wars threaten material sourcing for manufacturing companies. While these trade disputes often seem like geopolitical maneuvers between governments, their effects trickle down to everyday consumers in the form of higher prices, reduced availability of certain products, and potential job losses in affected industries. They may have a direct impact on the end consumer being able to buy what they want, when they want it, and at a price they can afford.

In addition to concerns about pricing and availability, geopolitical tensions can also create reputational risks depending on the labor practices, government policies, and instability of the country or region supplying the goods. For example, a supplement manufacturer may face backlash from sourcing its herbs from overharvested regions, like maca from Peru. Clothing and toy manufacturers have and continue to face backlash when sourcing from factories in China that permit exploitative labor practices. Consumers are demanding more transparency into the sourcing practices of manufacturers to understand where their products are coming from. A 2024 survey from PwC titled "Voices of the Consumer" revealed that approximately 85 percent of participants were willing to pay a "sustainability premium" for their sustainably produced or sourced products. However, the survey also found that consumers were only amenable to this premium so long as the cost didn't increase above 9.7 percent. This leaves sourcing professionals with the challenge of weighing potential risk and reputation against material costs when choosing suppliers.

The fourth driver of stress and duress is the constantly evolving landscape of emerging technology. The tech divide between manufacturing companies continues to widen as some companies, like Apple, strive to be on the forefront of procurement technology while others hope that their teams can continue to make do with their Excel spreadsheets and Outlook emails. The interesting thing is that the previous three stressors (cost-avoidance, supplier relationships, and geopolitical tensions) can be mitigated by technology. Digitization and data contextualization can create a competitive advantage. If a manufacturer can identify more supplier options in the market, they have more choices. More choices mean more negotiating power and reduced risk. In today's volatile supply chain environment, companies must go beyond reactive sourcing approaches. They require proactive, prescriptive solutions that not only analyze historical trends but also anticipate future challenges.

This is also a time when procurement teams are being forced to manage inventory in new ways. In previous decades, when there wasn't as much competition for materials and margins weren't as thin, manufacturing companies could afford to buy and hold excess raw materials or parts inventory. Toyota is credited with the shift to just-in-time (JIT) manufacturing in the 1970s, where companies would only buy the raw materials they could use to save on inventory storage costs. The growth of tech companies, however, perpetuated the need for JIT systems as companies found that their excess inventory was becoming obsolete. This lean strategy seemed like an ideal solution to manage costs until COVID hit. The pandemic exposed vulnerabilities in this approach as companies faced shortages and delays due to supply chain disruptions.

As a result, inventory levels have experienced wild pendulum swings in a post-COVID world. The pandemic underscored the importance of resilience over cost minimization. Many companies have shifted away from JIT toward just-in-case (JIC) inventory strategies. This shift involves holding higher inventory levels as a buffer against potential disruptions. The experience of sudden shortages and the inability to meet demand has led to a more cautious approach, with businesses stocking up on essential parts and materials to ensure continuity. Over-ordering can meet immediate business needs but often leads to excess inventory challenges. However, companies may find these challenges more manageable than the risks associated with under-ordering.

Unfortunately, these inventory challenges are not always well-known or well-understood by other departments within an organization. As a result, sourcing teams often face intense pressures from teams in finance, product development, engineering, or other areas of supply chain management. Sourcing professionals end up directing the majority of their focus to the top 20 percent of strategic suppliers to try and negotiate the most favorable terms. It is not for lack of wanting to work with more suppliers. The reality is that most sourcing teams do not have the capacity to foster deeper relationships with more of the suppliers they manage. Supplier relationship management is still a highly manual process that requires the direct involvement of sourcing specialists.

What do sourcing teams need to make better inventory management decisions? The first would be investments in advanced inventory management systems that offer real-time visibility and analytics. They need to utilize technology tools to get control of spending and to operationalize the best price and lead times for materials. They also need collaboration across the supply chain. Companies need to foster strong relationships from their suppliers to their customers to enhance communication and coordination. Information must be shared across companies to ensure that inventory levels align with demand fluctuations. Instead, sourcing teams are stretching the technology systems they currently have to the limits of their capacity. Many of the systems in use today simply aren't scalable to meet the needs of direct material sourcing.

Many of today's companies have shifted to a Software-as-a-Service, or SaaS, approach to technology. SaaS is a cloud-based technology model that allows companies to subscribe to tech software as needed across their enterprise. The shift to SaaS means that programs can now be accessed over the internet rather than requiring installation and storage on local computers. In the SaaS world, maintenance and updates are provided constantly by the software vendor. SaaS programs like Google Workspace and Microsoft 365 have been a godsend for companies looking for highly scalable software solutions. But SaaS has shortcomings when it comes to supporting sourcing teams that have complex data issues.

And so, these inventory problems persist. Finance continues to get angry about spending and inventory costs. Product development continues to sweat about what types of parts are being brought used in new product introduction. And sales teams are anxious to make sure that they'll be able to deliver what they promise their customers. Companies are now seeking ways to offload some of this labor and decision making to computers. This goes beyond the basic use of AI; we're now entering an era of the new agentic effect on business workflows.

AI agents are disrupting the world of SaaS. Chances are, if you've worked in or with procurement departments, you've been in a meeting that has shared what's known as a "spider map"—a visual representation of the data flow and suppliers or software that a company uses across various workflows. They are often overwhelming slides with hundreds of company logos and lines surrounding a central hub made up of a company's primary procurement systems. Spider maps represent the tech ecosystem of the company and may cover areas like identity verification programs, commodity insight programs, supplier scorecards, ESG measurements, bid analysis, and raw material sourcing.

Spider maps can be used to visually represent the SaaS

programs that procurement teams are working with. Their complexity does not necessarily mean that they're inefficient or ineffective. In fact, SaaS was a welcome and much-needed upgrade that addressed the shortcomings of procurement suites that tried to provide a company's S2P tools within one program. But SaaS has its own challenges, with individual software programs not interfacing with each other, keeping data siloed within certain groups or organizations within a company.

Whether you're a die-hard SaaS fan or you're indifferent to it, the reality is that technology and the new Agentic Notion in AI is moving beyond it. Like Blackberry when it refused to give up its keyboard for the new touchscreen technology in phones, those companies holding on to old technology may find themselves obsolete in the coming years. We are seeing evidence of these shifts in SaaS already, with slowed (or even declining) investment in SaaS companies. Newly funded companies must put forward a strategy that clearly embraces AI and federates their product to play in an agentic world.

What does it mean to transition to an Agentic Notion in procurement spaces? Agentic AI uses sophisticated reasoning and iterative planning to autonomously solve complex, multi-step problems. These systems ingest vast amounts of data from multiple data sources and third-party applications to independently analyze challenges, develop strategies, and execute tasks. More importantly, agentic AI has the potential for a level of autonomy that empowers "agents" to drive results with minimal human intervention. This means that repetitive, time-intensive tasks like supplier outreach, bid analysis, and spend optimization can be delegated to AI agents. These systems don't just analyze data; they act on it, automatically reordering raw materials, renegotiating contracts, or even pivoting sourcing strategies in response to disruptions.

Agentic AI is currently a complex and crowded area that is literally getting easier to develop and deploy by the day. At present it requires both user expertise and a deep level of AI sophistication. Agentic AI uses a four-step process for problem solving:

1. Perceive: AI agents gather and process data from various sources, such as sensors, databases, and digital interfaces. This involves extracting meaningful features, recognizing objects, or identifying relevant entities in the environment.

2. Reason: A large language model (a deep learning algorithm for large data sets) acts as the orchestrator, or reasoning engine, that understands tasks, generates solutions, and coordinates specialized models for specific functions like content creation, visual processing, or recommendation systems. This step uses techniques like retrieval-augmented generation (RAG), a software architecture that bridges large language models to proprietary, business-specific data sources, to deliver accurate and relevant outputs.

3. Act: By integrating with external tools and software via application programming interfaces, agentic AI can quickly execute tasks based on the plans it has formulated. Guardrails can be built into AI agents to help ensure they execute tasks correctly. For example,

a customer service AI agent may be able to process claims up to a certain amount, while claims above the amount would have to be approved by a human.

4. Learn: Agentic AI continuously improves through a feedback loop, or "data flywheel," where the data generated from its interactions is fed into the system to enhance models. This ability to adapt and become more effective over time offers businesses a powerful tool for driving better decision making and operational efficiency.

Understanding what agentic AI can achieve is more important than understanding how it works. This capability is particularly relevant in today's sourcing landscape, where agility and resilience are paramount. Supply chain disruptions, geopolitical instability, and inflationary pressures demand sourcing solutions that not only react but proactively anticipate and adapt. Agentic AI can deliver strategic decision making by integrating real-time data, predictive analytics, and autonomous execution into a seamless, self-reinforcing system. AI-powered platforms offer real-time market intelligence, location awareness insights, lead time insights, and risk assessment at the individual manufacturer part number (MPN) level. These insights can then be translated into decision-making workflows, creating a system that doesn't just inform but also acts. For example, a spend intelligence engine could identify cost-saving opportunities and execute supplier negotiations.

Moving to agentic AI means taking what used to be people-powered processes and decisions and shifting them to machine-based learning. It does not mean getting rid of sourcing or procurement teams all together. Instead, it opens their available bandwidth to lean into the areas that need human interaction and intelligence: setting goals and developing strategies; cultivating supplier relationships; managing stakeholder expectations; and completing complex negotiations. This means a major mental shift for many sourcing professionals whose business-as-usual work is spent bogged down in spreadsheets and disparate data systems. Agentic AI has the ability to revolutionize the day-to-day work of sourcing teams. At the same time, I can't help thinking of the Taoist parable of determining whether something is good or bad. Our perspective of a situation changes with time. What is a given, however, is that agentic AI in procurement is here and we need to address it.

When we're out on the open water, we do not have control of the timing or size of the waves that are coming our way. That doesn't mean, however, that we're completely out of control and have to tread water while we wait to get pummeled by the next wave. There are ways to anticipate the waves and flow with them rather than fight against them. The same is true for technology. We can stay afloat with our awareness of what's coming and our ability to adapt to it. The right technology can act like a buoy, allowing us to keep our heads above water and give us a line of sight at what's headed our way. Old technology can be like cement shoes that drag us to the bottom. I have always been surprised by the amount of people who choose to wear the shoes and keep their obsolete systems in place.

FOUR

THE FORMATION OF THE DATA GULCH

Have you ever watched the reality TV show *Survivor*? Launched back in May 2000, the show places a handful of contestants in a remote location. They have to figure out their own food, shelter, and how to make fire, among other challenges randomly presented to them to whittle down the number of participants. On *Survivor*, winning isn't determined by someone's size or six-pack abs; it is about strategy and resilience. It reminds me of the current state of sourcing. That's not to say that historically strategy and resilience didn't matter, but there is little to compare to the rate of change and the number of factors that are involved in most sourcing businesses today.

COVID-19 ushered in a new era of survival mode for manufacturers, shifting them away slightly from lean cost-saving techniques and toward resilience. What can we do to prevent the experience of shortages and delays again? Evaluating risk became even more of a hot topic during this time. Sourcing companies wanted to do a better job of really knowing their suppliers and how they were setting themselves up for resilience—almost like building alliances on the *Survivor* to ensure they'd both make it to the end. When it came to addressing their resilience, though, companies started to see that one significant part of their struggle was making sense of their own data.

Data is generated every day. Almost every company over the past twenty years have not possessed the tools, collection processes, or ability to collect, examine, interpret, and turn this data into action. Modern day sourcing faces many of the data challenges that other parts of a company face, from finance and marketing to sales and product development. However, the issue is heightened for sourcing teams because much of the sourcing data in the past was lost, not captured or simply not mined. There wasn't really a word to describe this problem that I encountered at all manufacturing companies, from European multi-billion-euro revenue firms to the small, nimble sub-one hundred million-dollar company. I decided to create a term that encompasses the problem: the Data Gulch. I've witnessed this Data Gulch phenomenon, where the sheer size and magnitude of the data is overwhelming for sourcing professionals to try to turn into insights. It's a real problem that we can name and it's causing businesses real pain. Put on your colored bandanas, contestants. This terrain is rough!

If I asked you to envision a gulch, what would come to mind? If you're a fan of old Western movies, chances are you're envisioning a deadly ravine filled with swirls of dust and the occasional spiky cactus. Overhead might be a near-constant circling of buzzards. If you're more the water-loving type, like me, you may envision something like the Tonga or Mariana Trench, a dark abyss filled with unknown creatures. Regardless of the setting of your gulch, chances are it has two features: 1) it's massive; and 2) if you're in it, you're probably in some sort of trouble.

A gulch isn't created overnight. In geology, most gulches are formed due to gradual erosion over a long period of time. Heavy rainfalls, melting snow, or even small creeks continually wear away at the soil or rock, creating channels that deepen and widen with time. Just a few hundred to a few thousand to a few million years later, you have massive changes to the topography of the land thanks to the introduction of water to the space.

Data gulches do not take nearly as long to form. Each piece of software or tech solution that is added to the company acts like water to the soil, carving out more channels for data to accumulate. Having data is most often a good thing. It allows us to analyze what is happening, look for trends, and make decisions. Too much data (particularly if it is not contextualized into a format we can interpret and make decisions from) ends up acting like a dark place. Your visibility becomes limited.

The proliferation of data compounds the very data gulch that gives sourcing so much trouble. In 2010, the world generated approximately two zettabytes of data. By 2023, this figure had surged to 120 zettabytes, marking a sixty-fold increase in just over a decade. Projections indicate that by the end of 2025, global data creation will reach 181 zettabytes.

Like a desertscape or an undersea world, supply chains are their own ecosystems and operate in various states of growth and decay, though unlike desert woodrats or phytoplankton, the supply chain ecosystem is made up of things like cost savings, vendor collaboration, and new product introduction. It includes tools like parts/cost master sheets, supplier performance review, and negotiating playbooks. And it utilizes programs like ERP systems for contracts, business intelligence forecasts, and supply chain planning systems for supply planning, demand planning, and operational planning. The supply chain ecosystem is complex and vibrant, with many moving parts that interact or rely on each other.

To support this ecosystem, most modern companies have a sizable procurement platform stack. The platform stack includes all the software programs and services a company uses to manage its processes and workflows. Take, for example, the risk component of the supply chain ecosystem. Within the genus of risk, you could have several species, such as compliance, risk monitoring, reputational risk, and risk score. Each of these might require its own system, like Interos for risk monitoring and Rapid Ratings for financial risk. When you multiply the systems by the number of species in the supply chain ecosystem, you might end up with tens to hundreds of programs to manage.

In addition to having to manage each system, supply chain teams need to be aware that each system also produces results that meet the objectives or goals of the user. For example, if my role at a company is to evaluate suppliers for risk, I will be using data from my risk management programs to select the suppliers with the lowest risk scores. That may put me at odds with the engineering team, which prefers to have a certain part, made of a certain material, that comes from a specific supplier, regardless of their risk. And that information might be at odds with what the finance team is willing to spend on the shipping costs from either of these countries of origin when a comparable supplier is located nearby. There is so much data to inform decision-making, yet it rarely lines up with the goal that is in the best interest of the company.

The result is that companies find themselves drowning in solutions. To handle the flood of data that the '90s and '00s brought us and continue to bring us, we respond by over-tooling, over-subscribing, over-architecting, and over-peopling to manage all of it. The result is that companies overspend and under-save. Being "over it" may be what brought you to this book in the first place.

I have found that three primary steps form a Data Gulch in a business. Historically, siloed data is held captive in a variety of enterprise systems. It starts with data tools. When companies start, they might hire a person and give them a spreadsheet system, like Excel or Sheets, and a mail system like Outlook. They might add tools like Microsoft Power BI or Tableau to produce some fancy reports. With increases in product demand, the company hires more people who create more spreadsheets, emails, and reports. Everything feels like it's doing what it needs to do, but with time the data gets really complex. The tools do not have the ability to keep data current and refreshed—at least not without people power to make all the changes. The waters start to get unclear.

Then companies find a solution. They often buy information from companies like Z2Data, Silicon Expert Technologies, or HIS Accuris. These programs provide benchmarking for parts. Companies are essentially buying data points to make sense of all the data they've collected. They've unknowingly entered the second stage of Data Gulch formation. To make sense of overwhelming data, they've created more data.

By now the company is swimming in a large amount of data. While there may be spots of light or visibility, all the data leaves a lot of people and teams in the dark. They can see what's in front of them but don't have the same visibility to see what other teams or departments do. To solve for this, companies invest in data storage. This is where you get data solutions like warehouses, lakes, mesh, or fabric. They are centralized repositories where all the data gets dumped with the hope that it will build cross-company visibility. But in that massive sea of data, it can be a real challenge to know what you're fishing for. You are now existing in the Data Gulch.

At this point, companies often realize that they are out of most tech market solutions to solve their massive data problems. Companies that have faced procurement data chaos typically throw up their hands at the data problem. Often internal IT and external consultants shift modalities to try and use technology band-aids to understand areas of their data abyss. They might hire a few technologists who try to write custom applications to make sense of the information. Unfortunately, by the time most coders try to integrate eight to ten data sources, they tap out and fail.

Many companies have tried to address the Data Gulch and had mixed results. General Electric, a multinational conglomerate, implemented a centralized procurement data

model. Their well-recorded project included data dedupli-
cation and normalization tools to merge duplicate supplier
records, along with establishing a global taxonomy for materials, parts, and services to standardize descriptions across
regions. The goal was to gain better visibility into supplier
relationships (which they did) and enable faster sourcing
decisions (which they did not).

When companies experience "dirty" data, or data quality
issues, it's like underwater volcanoes erupting in the Mariana
Trench: the deepest gulch gets more unstable. One well-known
example of this comes from Ford, a leading US-based automo-
bile manufacturer. Ford spent years and tens of millions of dollars on modernization and data analytics projects. They exe-
cuted plans to migrate large repositories of legacy data into a
unified platform, but significant data quality issues surfaced,
leading to delays and massive cost overruns. The lack of standardized data formats across these legacy systems resulted in
integration challenges, compounded by dirty data and impacting decision-making processes and operational efficiency.

People are well-intentioned, but they are outmatched with
the complexity of data. This is not an area in which you can be
a tech generalist and figure it out. This type of work requires a
true tech specialist who has achieved a niche, narrow, but deep
understanding of how to work with this data complexity—
someone who can work with over one hundred data sources
of asymmetric information and translate it into a usable form.
It explains why Apple can afford to handle this in-house while
most other manufacturing companies cannot.

What does this Data Gulch actually mean for companies? The Data Gulch manifests itself at companies through the Decision Abyss, where misaligned interests and asymmetric information occur, leading to less effective decision making for companies. This challenge in making data-driven decisions means that there is a loss of sourcing optimization. And because sourcing optimization opportunities exist at each stage of a product life cycle, from initial development through eventual decline, it means that far more money is being spent per product than is needed. So many companies miss savings opportunities because the needed information is hidden in the dark, murky territory of the Data Gulch.

Supply chain is not the only back-office workflow that experiences the Data Gulch. Airbus, one of the world's largest aircraft manufacturers, launched the One ERP initiative to integrate multiple legacy ERP systems into a unified platform. This company used data lakes and middleware solutions to aggregate procurement data from different business units, powering real-time supplier tracking. With this single source of truth, this manufacturer could pivot quickly to alternative suppliers during supply chain disruptions.

Having and storing more data has never been the solution, but having the data and having the capacity to blend it and utilize it in a way that allows manufacturers to make better buying decisions is. Contextualizing the data in the Data Gulch to create information that can be used for decision making means that companies have the opportunity to better manage cash and predict outcomes when it comes to building products.

When companies allow the Data Gulch to form (which is almost inevitable given the systems currently available in procurement), it means that the companies' rich natural resources (money and associates' time) are being allowed to float down into the depths. Companies that clean and streamline their procurement data reduce sourcing delays, improve cost efficiencies, and strengthen supplier resilience. Those that don't struggle with slow, costly, and reactive procurement decisions—especially during supply chain disruptions. If their data is in the Gulch, it becomes out of reach. If so much value is lost, why don't companies invest more time and resources in getting their sourcing data in order?

The answer is that it's not that easy. There are other enterprise challenges at play that present very real obstacles for improving the quality of supply chain data and the ease at which supply chain professionals can work. We'll explore these ship-wrecking barrier reefs in the next section.

SECTION 2

SWIMMING AGAINST THE CURRENT

FIVE

Why Sourcing Teams Struggle to Get Money for THEIR Projects

Analyzing the intricacies of sourcing data is far from enjoyable. Most people might find it somewhere in the similar "fun" range of getting a lobster-red sunburn on the first day of your vacation or listening to static on the radio when you road-trip through a remote area. There is a pain factor to them all. Most tools on the market today for sourcing data analysis lack a key feature: the ability to make easy, data-driven decisions. But like SPF 50 sunscreen for skin protection or Spotify for radio-free zones, there actually *are* tools out there that can ease the pain of analyzing sourcing data. So why aren't companies buying them?

There are several factors at play, but most of them lead back to how the human mind works. When a company is making the decision to buy or not buy software, they often take four factors into consideration: time to value (TTV), time to obsolescence, scalability, and ROI. TTV refers to the length of time it will take after purchase to implement and realize value for the company. When facing these four factors (and the very real prospect of taking multiple years and millions of dollars to begin addressing the problems), many companies simply do not pass the TTV gate. Fear paralyzes them.

These long TTV programs stoke a new fear and the second buying factor: time to obsolescence. There is a far greater risk factor when investing in a technology that could take years to fully implement, particularly given the speed of technological evolution just in the past decade. Complex problems rarely have simple solutions, and the Data Gulch is most definitely a complex problem.

Scalability is another consideration, particularly for companies experiencing rapid growth. There are programs that simply don't work once a company has reached a certain size or level of complexity. I have seen many companies try to triage the programs they have, like Excel, to stretch its capabilities and scale beyond the size it is meant to manage. Unfortunately, the "use it until it breaks" mentality is not as cost-effective for software as it is for your teenager's car or your TV set at home. In software, stretching programs beyond their limits sets teams up for slower running speeds and more system crashes. Instead of getting business as usual taken care of, teams become part-time tech support trying to get their technology to work for their most basic needs...

...which brings us to ROI. Are we getting our money's worth and more from the programs we invest in? Perhaps with numerous bespoke, stand-alone solutions you are trying something. But squeezing every last bit of functionality out of these solutions before having to upgrade often leads to a tangled data mess. ROI is more than just the hard cost of buying and maintaining the program, otherwise known as your "hard ROI."

The other piece is "soft ROI," or the intangibles and harder-to-account-for returns to a program.

Soft ROI may include things like the supplier relationship opportunities created from sourcing professionals having more available time to invest in partnerships rather than figure out why their spreadsheet isn't doing its thing that day. Soft ROI may be your team's attrition rate or morale. Do people feel enabled to do their job with the tools you're providing them or is a portion of their time spent engaged in their own personal tech battle day after day?

One last important piece to soft ROI is a company's net promoter score (NPS). The NPS is a measure of how likely your customer is to recommend you. Although the term may not be commonly emphasized in sourcing, we recognize that fostering strong relationships with our suppliers is vital. These partnerships are essential to securing timely access to what we need and play a crucial role in swiftly resolving any challenges that arise. In today's global economy, this relationship building is perhaps more important than ever. Your technology investments have an impact on that.

So why do companies choose to invest hundreds of thousands to millions of dollars in technology for some departments and not others? Why is the value of a purchase for the marketing team's need to reach customers given priority over the sourcing team's supplier relationships needed to make the products? The first factor comes from what I hypothesize is a greater dopamine hit from tools that grow revenue over tools that minimize cost. While savvy company owners and investors look at all parts of the profit and loss, revenue growth is the king and queen. It makes sense then that companies would be more inclined to invest a greater amount of money in revenue-generating systems or departments. It's hard ROI winning over soft ROI.

We see this when companies invest in expensive and complex CRMs for their sales teams to find leads, schedule appointments, and automate customer follow-up. Sales relationships are given high priority because the return is clear and easy to measure. As such, sales teams are primarily evaluated on their sales revenue. Tools that make their lives easier and free up time for more sales opportunities are a relatively easy sell to most company executives, including financial officers.

The same can be said for marketing systems that can track the performance of campaigns. Companies may look to evaluate their click-through rate (CTR) or customer acquisition cost (CAC). They'll look at web traffic and social media engagement and the related conversion rates. It's the exciting part of business: launching creative campaigns and following the results.

Even in non-revenue generating departments, such as finance, many companies are inclined to invest in expensive financial reporting tools. Why? Because it's the window to revenue. It's the visibility and granularity of the company's financial position that is so vital to the functioning of the company. Shareholders demand visibility. Leadership across departments is often evaluated based, at least in part, on the financial results they've delivered. Financial software investments just seem to make sense, and so they get the funding to purchase what they need. (After all, they're most often the department that decides what everyone else is able to spend).

I equate the value of contextualizing data to that of being able to collect gold from the ocean. According to the National Oceanic Service there is an estimated 20 million tons of gold dissolved in the ocean and deposited in rocks on the sea floor. We don't realize it and can't collect it, though, because it's in extremely low concentrations or too deep for us to extract with today's machinery. For companies swimming in the Data Gulch of sourcing information, trying to find and derive meaning from the data pieces may feel almost as impossible as trying to collect oceanic gold. You can't do it if you don't have the right tool.

For companies that do not understand the value of this data for direct material sourcing, it's hard to generate excitement with anyone across the company. They don't realize the gold is there. They cannot understand the benefits of aggregating this data for improved decision intelligence because until now, there weren't really tools to mine the data in a meaningful way.

Success in direct material sourcing technology is really about enhancing the company's decision intelligence. I find decision intelligence, bringing together broad sets of data to drive better decision making and decision support, to be fascinating. As it turns out, I am not the only one who thinks this way and am likely in good company with you, the reader. My company, LevaData, conducted a global study involving chief procurement officers and executive sourcing leaders. Approximately 44 percent of the people we engaged with were in Europe, 17 percent in North America, and the remainder spread between the Asian Pacific, Middle East, and Africa.

We learned that the top companies embrace decision intelligence and are leading with it to engage those outside of procurement in supply chain and in engineering and product design. They use that engagement to drive efficiency and to be better stewards inside of their company. Through decision intelligence, greater things happen—more people get together and actually make better decisions. Things like third party risk, supplier visibility, and parts awareness bubble to the top as priorities for decision making for all these leaders.

If top-performing companies value decision intelligence in direct material sourcing, then why isn't every manufacturing company using it? The reality is that this is an incredibly challenging endeavor, requiring significant effort and dedication. Many companies have explored various solutions, yet most have achieved little to no success in overcoming their data issues. There is an immense frustration, and sometimes even jobs on the line, when companies invest resources in trying to solve the problem with very little luck in moving the needle.

Many companies desire a solution to the Decision Abyss, whether they realize it or not. Unfortunately, without a clear understanding of how their Decision Abyss formed and the fact that it is like the tip of an iceberg with a tremendous Data Gulch existing below the surface, they approach the problem with ineffective, incomplete solutions. Smaller manufacturers may recognize the challenge in bringing their data together and contextualizing it for decision making. The solutions sold to them (or that they buy into simply because they're so commonplace) are things like Microsoft Excel, Google Sheets, and other general-purpose intelligence tools like Power BI and Tableau.

Dashboards seem great at first, acting as one seemingly single source of truth that provides a clear look at the data that is available. Data visualization feels really good. The dashboard makes it seem like we've captured the full picture of what we're looking at, featuring things like "power queries" for data extraction and "natural language queries" so that you don't have to speak tech to find what you're looking for. It's not surprising that teams can become enchanted with the idea of a dashboard being a real visual problem solver.

But is this dashboard really helping you make better decisions or is it just giving you a point of view? Is it simply taking the disparate data you have and displaying it in a nice visual without truly evaluating for risk, cost, availability, or any other factors that you need to be aware of? Is it taking into account sourcing data that is out there in the world or only the sourcing data you have managed to collect? Rather than improve a company's data intelligence, many tech tools simply create more data for the company, enlarging the Data Gulch even further.

Dashboards can often feel like madness. With each movement forward, companies find themselves plunging deeper into the problem rather than finding their way out of it. What is even more frustrating to many is that the problem of direct material sourcing seems like it *should* be solvable. Indirect material purchasing, like laptops you need to buy for your team in bulk to get a good price break, is easy. Indirect material purchasing for all the items that make a company run is relatively straightforward.

But direct material sourcing, the parts and materials you need to make your products, is incredibly complex due to the number of factors and considerations at hand. Financial decision-makers outside of procurement may not understand the difference between indirect material sourcing and direct material sourcing, so they're treated the same when it comes to tech investments. Companies will try to dump their data into a data warehouse or data repository, hoping their IT team can write some extraction scripts to turn the data into insights.

The problem is that many companies hire tech generalists to support the company. These are often people who have experience across several tech areas and can perform a multitude of tech tasks to varying degrees. Don't get me wrong—companies need tech generalists to handle many of their everyday IT tasks. But a tech generalist should be viewed like a boat captain who has experience driving many styles and sizes of boats. If you pass that captain a single-person, deep-diving submarine, they likely will have no idea what to do.

At the same time, those singularly focused deeper divers of technology rarely get hired by companies because their focus is so limited and specialized. Chances are they'd be sitting at a desk playing Candy Crush for weeks or months until you needed to call on them for another exploratory data dive down to the specific manufacturing part number level. Hiring many geeked-out tech specialists within a company does not make financial sense.

It's no wonder that companies may be extra trigger-shy to invest in sourcing technology. They try and things don't work out as planned. They think they've found the solution, and then they fall hard. I've coined two terms for this buying phenomenon: The Apex of Love and the Trough of Despair. The Apex of Love is that point just before a contract to buy the next new program or solution is signed. It comes after all the research, comparisons, negotiating, and approvals. It's when the buyer shifts from the logical side of purchasing to the emotion-driven side. They have their solution, and they are in love with it.

As soon as the ink is dry, the clock starts, and the buyer wants the program to deliver. It's at this point they enter the Trough of Despair—the immediate regret, remorse, or letdown from their decision. Perhaps it's then that they notice the icons on the program aren't big enough, or the color of what they ordered wasn't quite right. The dopamine high has worn off and now they're looking for any footholds of hope to help them climb out of this trough and back to the Apex of Love.

This emotional climb, fall, and slow escape seems to be more severe when it comes to sourcing programs, thanks to their historically long TTV factors. Whereas ROI may have been the primary driver in the initial purchasing decision, TTV becomes the most important metric after the purchase is made. Unfortunately, most of these programs do not deliver fast results. For example, everyone (okay, maybe not *everyone*) has dreams of supply chain planning improvements like Sales & Operations Execution (S&OE) or Sales & Operations Planning (S&OP) processes. These long-tail projects often take several years and significant expense for companies to build, modify, test, and eventually cut over to a new system. In the meantime, the Chief Supply Chain

Officer has to justify why these long-tail investments are good investments. It's a real challenge to do if you don't have some short-term wins and financial gains in the process.

The result is that rather than getting what they need and risk feeling that fall from the Apex of Love, companies and their sourcing departments opt to do the best they can with what they have. It's a Band-Aid-and-chewing gum approach to patching systems to get by as much as possible. Problems are temporarily solved, and sourcing professionals continue along with their work as best they can...until the next wave of disruption hits. It creates a feeling of hypervigilance and constant stress. But when you've been in it for so long, it just feels normal.

To solve the problems in a meaningful and effective way, we need to clearly state what the problems are: zero data integrity and almost no actionable insight that sourcing teams can act upon. These are two problems that may be hard for companies to admit. It's like when you ask someone how they're doing and they fold their arms across their chest and respond, "I'm fine." That's the answer they want you to hear, but everyone knows the truth. It's only when a company is willing to own that their direct materials process is broken, their email and spreadsheet workflow tools aren't cutting it anymore, their data is inconsistent or problematic, and that they can't get to the answers they really need that we can really get to work finding the solution.

When I presented at a sourcing conference with one of the leaders from a leading household manufacturing company, she mentioned what is perhaps the most challenging problem: people's willingness to do things differently. She mentioned how she could have the Ferrari of computer systems, but if her team was unwilling to even look at it or take it for a test drive, then it didn't matter if they had the system available to them. It often takes a strong-willed change agent who is willing to step up or step in and alter deeply ingrained behaviors. When most people step back from the ledge, it takes a leader with chutzpah to acknowledge when something is broken or could be done better.

One of our LevaData clients came to us (as most do) because they experienced a shock to their supply chain and someone stepped up to the plate to find a way to work smarter. We provided a solution that contextualized the data of this $9 billion manufacturing company with a TTV of just sixty days, giving them a system of record to compare the price, risk, transportation costs, tariffs, and other factors of their parts. In turn, they now negotiate their parts prices on a monthly basis, rather than quarterly or semiannually, because they have the up-to-date decision intelligence to use as leverage. As a result, they've enhanced their cost savings and are using it to fund the long-tail projects that their department needs.

But this senior supply chain executive doesn't always come along or step up. Sometimes procurement doesn't get the new, shiny program because nobody in procurement feels compelled to ask for it. This is something I find fascinating, given that the role of procurement is primarily finding and purchasing things. Like the chef who never cooks at home or the massage therapist who never gets a massage themselves, it appears that procurement teams spend so much time buying for everyone else that they don't buy for themselves.

In some ways, procurement teams are also the worst to sell to because they are expert negotiators. They will remove every frill, bell, and whistle in the name of cost savings. If it feels extraneous or unnecessary, they make do without it.

Perhaps it's because they have made do for so long with what they have and that working at a "hair on fire" pace has become so normal that they barely notice the burn anymore. Or perhaps they don't understand the true ROI that investing in a procurement program could provide, both in hard ROI in the form of cost savings and soft ROI in the form of improved allocation of time and increase in employee job satisfaction. I believe that the lack of investment in part has to do with the fact that procurement has had a more conservative approach to investing in themselves. In some ways they're held to an even higher ROI standard than other departments because they are procurement people and they measure everything. Their standard for what they buy is higher than so many of the other traditional automation projects.

My hunch is that there is also a bit of a mental framework at play that doesn't want to admit there is a problem. After all, many procurement departments do find solutions eventually for each supply chain disruption they experience. They do figure out a way to make it work, regardless of whether their staffing is cut or their budget shrinks. Procurement almost always gets it done. They are often the unsung heroes of the company.

In some ways it makes sense that they wouldn't want to admit there is a problem. Admitting would mean that something would have to change. Nobody likes the thought of their job being automated, even though the reality of AI is that many jobs (including those that involve complex decision making) can be taken over by AI.

The thing about procurement, however, is that incorporating AI doesn't mean the role would be eliminated. There needs to be a mindset shift in viewing AI in businesses as an "either/or"—as in, "Either I keep working away at this job in a painstaking and unsustainable way" or, "I let AI do the work and I'm out of a job!" AI is not an "either/or"; it's an "and." You can let AI absorb the tedium and mental load of the multitude of tiny choices you're forced to deal with, *and* you now have the capacity to work differently. Your role will evolve. The problems that sapped so much of your brain power can now be done by computers, leaving your human intelligence to things like negotiation, building relationships, and innovating connections across departments.

Altering human behavior is a formidable challenge. It's only when we experience significant discomfort, like struggling with a plain hammer instead of a nail gun during construction, that we become willing or compelled to embrace change. Change is also hard because it means identifying that something needs to change. It entails raising our hand and saying, "I need help." That wasn't easy to do as a kid and certainly doesn't get easier when your pay is riding on it. And so, people continue with their spreadsheets because that feels like comfort or security. It's pretty reliable and gets the job done. It's choosing to drive the Hyundai Accent when the Ferrari SF90 Stradale is also sitting in the garage. New AI procurement solutions are not a disruption to the system—they are the evolution toward better decision intelligence.

When you take a step back, it's widely recognized that sales professionals rely on CRM systems to perform at their best. Similarly, in the world of finance, it's generally accepted that CFOs and controllers need ERP platforms to manage their responsibilities. But when it comes to procurement (especially direct material sourcing), the same clarity doesn't exist. There's no shared understanding that these professionals deserve a dedicated system tailored to their needs, akin to a CRM or ERP.

Instead, they're often expected to deliver more with less—under pressure, with limited tools, and while navigating complex collaboration with IT and traditional supply chain functions. It's a demanding, often unsustainable position. And unless someone is willing to challenge the status quo, it remains an unwinnable game.

To begin your journey into decision intelligence, you must take that first step. Approach your data with curiosity and determination, and realize what's possible if you have contextualized, well-understood data. Going down this road is like building a bridge over the Decision Abyss. It doesn't happen overnight. You have to start one block at a time, one crane at a time, one day at a time.

I don't know where the future lies, but I know that LevaData knows more about parts, ingredients, and metals than anybody else. We have more sources of that data and how we bring that to life is almost industry-agnostic. If you care about that information, there's not going to be a better source on the planet. In the pursuit of decision intelligence, you'll start to see the Decision Abyss shrink. You'll begin to engage others, particularly in engineering and in supply chain, and you'll start driving better decision making. You'll become an even greater asset to your organization. This should not create fear, uncertainty, and doubt. It should fire you up for what is possible!

SIX

PRIORITIZING LEAKS IN THE BOAT

John Wooden was a US collegiate basketball coach known as "the Wizard of Westwood" due to his unprecedented winning streak with the UCLA Bruins. During his time as coach, Wooden led the team to a record ten National Collegiate Athletic Association (NCAA) National Championship wins—twice as many as the next coach on the all-time list. Under his leadership, the Bruins also set the NCAA record with an eighty-eight-game winning streak. What was it about Wooden's coaching strategy that led the team to such an unparalleled level of success?

Wooden's view of his role as coach was to take the millions of different components that go into winning a game and align them to a single vision. That meant that while each player had their own individual talents and desire to be recognized for them, it was more important for them to be aligned with the goal of the team winning by playing together. Wooden said, "It is amazing how much can be accomplished if no one cares who gets the credit."

Is it possible to replicate Wooden's leadership style in sourcing and supply chain? In a world of KPIs and performance reviews, it may be more challenging to keep employees and departments focused on the overall vision of the company. What can result, however, are competing priorities impacting decision making. What is best for one department might not be for another, or for the company as a whole. It's akin to being a ball hog that wants to dominate on the court at the expense of one's teammates and the team as a whole. You become the best player on the worst team—a short-sighted approach to career success. How do companies motivate employees toward the goal of making the right decisions for the company over their own personal recognition, particularly when their career and professional reputation is involved?

To grasp this concept, it's essential to examine the operational dynamics of various departments within a company and identify key factors that influence their decision-making processes. In my experience, with nearly all departments, there is often a greater drive to make money *now* rather than later— and this is particularly true at the executive leadership level. On average, many company executives only plan on being in their role for three to five years before changing departments or changing companies all together. And who would blame them? Leaders may be formally or informally evaluated on a monthly, quarterly, semi-annual, and annual basis to ensure they are driving results and delivering quickly. It compels them to score short-term financial wins to demonstrate their leadership skills.

Choosing the short game at the expense of the long game is a short-sighted approach to running a company, though. The short game highlights the skills of the individual to innovate and implement quickly. In some departments, that works.

In others, like supply chain management and direct material sourcing, it can send the department deeper into a Data Gulch with short-term solutions buoying the team so they forget they're drowning. Supply chain and enterprise IT projects are long and complex, often taking at least two to three years to fully implement. And what if it doesn't work out as expected? It's understandable that leaders are less inclined to make long-term project bets.

In 2014, PwC released the results of a survey conducted by Booz & Company that surveyed sixty chief information officers (CIOs), an executive position with a notoriously high turnover rate. "According to 70 percent of our respondents, the failure of a major IT project is one of the primary reasons that the tide turns against the CIO. And although failure doesn't always lead directly to dismissal, the interviews we conducted show that it is often a contributing factor. These projects are typically complex, expensive, multiyear enterprise programs involving new ERP, CRM, or core industry-specific solutions that promise to fundamentally change business performance and improve competitiveness."

When it comes to fixing long-term problems, some companies perform their own version of "jumping the shark." While I've heard this phrase for years, I became curious about its origin when writing this book. Jumping the shark originated from a 1977 episode of the series *Happy Days*. A popular TV show that had already experienced several years of success, *Happy Days* seemed to be running low on plot lines to engage the viewers' interest.

In this particular episode, the main character, Arthur Herbert Fonzarelli, better known as "Fonzie" or "The Fonz," is in his signature black leather jacket and is water skiing. As if that wasn't ridiculous enough of an image, the screenwriters turned the level of absurdity up a notch. They had Fonzie jump over a shark in the water while skiing. He literally jumped the shark, sparking a phrase for creative and business projects that appear to be struggling and begin resorting to absurd or thoughtless decisions.

I have seen many supply chain departments resort to their own version of jumping the shark when it comes to facing the challenge of the Data Gulch and the resulting Decision Abyss. In many of these cases, companies made major capital investments in technology and warehouses based on poor data or emotional decision making. One such company was General Motors in the 1980s when CEO Roger Smith relied on his love and fascination with technology to grow GM's investment in automation from 300 robots to nearly 14,000 new robots.

Like the image of Fonzie jumping over a shark, I'm sure the vision of new, largely automated factories probably seemed like a wow factor that would differentiate GM from its competitors at the time. Unfortunately, the robots never really worked, allegedly malfunctioning by painting themselves or dropping windshields onto car seats. Within a short time, GM scrapped the majority of the project, losing billions of dollars and significant market share to its more agile and lean competitors, Toyota and Nissan. Smith was removed from his position as CEO and the decision is regarded as one of the largest failures in US supply chain history.

The tech boom of the 1990s resulted in several other companies soaring to success, only to burst due to over-investment in technology that failed to deliver. Now relegated to the annals of dot com history, WebVan was once a thriving online grocery initiative that had the financial support of companies such as Goldman Sachs. Their IPO raised billions of dollars as they prepared to revolutionize the way people shopped for groceries, an industry with historically low profit margins that often range in the single digits. WebVan took their influx of capital and built several expensive, automated warehouses to handle anticipated demand.

Unfortunately, demand for their service never came close to the capacity that they built for. Within just a few years, WebVan saw their market capitalization go from billions of dollars to almost nothing. They ran out of capital before they ever found a way to increase consumer demand. As the old aphorism goes, WebVan was "using a hammer to kill a flea." They over-invested without having any data-driven evidence that their investment would generate a return. This is just another example of using the wrong tools for a job.

General Motors and WebVan are just two examples of major technology investment failures in supply chain management. There are thousands more, perhaps not so public or damaging, where companies have invested significant dollars in trying to improve their supply chain processes with little to no return. Given the long track record of technology project failures, it is no surprise that companies are apprehensive about investing in major, long-term solutions. When they do look at tech solutions, they're often driven toward solutions that address what feel like the most urgent or pervasive issues at the company. Supply chain processes, including manufacturing, transportation, and inventory management, are not generally at the top of the list when it comes to a company's greatest pain points. Consequently, sourcing professionals consistently achieve their ambitious goals despite having minimal resources, a challenge that intensifies with each passing year.

Within the supply chain organization itself, there are additional challenges of competing roles and the misalignment of incentives. A CEO or CFO may see the full picture of what the best choices or outcomes would be, however most supply chain decisions are not made at the CEO/CFO level. Instead, individual departments have the potential to operate like fiefdoms, each making decisions based on the data they have and the metrics by which they're evaluated.

The supply chain team may be looking at their sourcing group wondering why production hasn't started on the newest model of the product. They may not understand that the engineering team incorporated new parts that have longer lead times or require new contracts to be negotiated. Meanwhile, engineering is wondering why they're still seeing production of the previous product models. They may not understand the warehousing cost or scrap cost of not moving this old inventory before the newer products are sold.

Finance joins the party and wants to understand why the cost of goods sold is increasing, as inventory builds up or the new product design features more expensive parts. They may not see that the consumer market is demanding more bespoke, customized products that require more costly inputs. The consumer market is also driving obsolescence at a frenzied rate due to their demand for the next brightest and shiniest version, putting pressure on the sales team to try and move older models until the newer ones are ready. All eyes shift their gaze to sourcing and eagerly watch as sourcing professionals balance the chaos and make it happen.

Procurement teams are judged based on their cost management, their inventory levels, and their ability to deliver. At the same time, they are not the decision makers when it comes to the design of a product, nor do they have control over the sales and marketing of a product to consumers. When product designs change and new or different components are needed, it's a big deal for procurement. Working with new suppliers or switching suppliers means new contract language, new legal agreements, and fresh negotiations on payment terms and policies for starters. In a field where relationship management is so important, procurement works to find the balance between continuing with established suppliers while also trying to meet the engineering, cost, and delivery needs of other departments in their organization. They are basing these decisions off the best data available, which may not be the same data that other departments are working with to drive their decision-making process.

This brings us back to the Data Gulch. It's the chasm of data that leads to poor decision making or the Decision Abyss. With the overwhelming amount of data, it's not surprising that people only look at the data that matters most for them. I recall a meeting I once had with a sourcing associate where we used LevaData's tools to show him that his options for material parts sourcing were far greater than what his Excel spreadsheet of contacts and pricing he was working from implied.

We were delighted with our findings! When we contextualized the company's supplier data and plugged it in with our supplier resources, we found that by making a few changes he could save 10 percent on his spend. These savings, potentially compounding over months or years, could have huge, positive implications for the company. What we didn't anticipate was another barrier created by competing interests. The associate did not seem to share our excitement.

"Could we save maybe 2 percent for now?" he asked.

I was flabbergasted at the request. "You want to save... less?"

What I learned was that he had a target KPI of 2 percent savings. If he met that or went above it, he would receive his bonus. His bonus, however, was not based on how much he saved, just the fact that he achieved 2 percent savings or more. His concern was that while 10 percent would be great for the company, it might set him up for failure in future years by making it more difficult for him to achieve additional 2 percent savings down the road.

My jaw dropped. His concerns were valid. His personal incentives and the company incentives were not aligned. For this reason, he was only willing to make good decisions for the company rather than *great* decisions due to the way his compensation and job performance metrics were structured. I share his story because it's a microcosm of what can happen at a larger scale at all levels within an organization. Individuals do what's best for them rather than the team; teams do what's best for them rather than the department; departments do what's best for them rather than the company. And because they use offline processes, like spreadsheets and databases that not everyone has visibility into, these suboptimal decisions continue being made, with a compounding effect over time. The Decision Abyss deepens.

What if there were greater data transparency for that person's team and what if he didn't have to be the one to even make the decision on which supplier was best because AI data intelligence pointed him in the right direction? What if his compensation were based on a different metric—one that could not be performed by AI solutions? Extrapolate this through the business and you begin to see how companies can pull themselves out of the Decision Abyss when they have the right data to work with.

The modern supply chain leader needs to be willing to change to stay ahead of the curve. It starts by identifying and being honest with the actual issues of the organization. It means taking a critical eye to "the way we do things" to reimagine what is possible. It also means looking for misalignment of goals and priorities that can have a negative impact on driving long-term value. To gain a competitive advantage in today's supply chain sector, leaders have to predict what is coming and know how to respond.

Leaders have the ability to respond best when they're using a clear system of record, a single source of aggregated information that is consistent and accurate. Having a company-wide system of record allows the entire organization to have one viewpoint. To bring this back to our example of the employee who only wanted to save 2 percent when he could save 10 percent, having a single system of record rather than individually siloed sources of data would mean that everyone would have line of sight into the data he was using for his decision making. He would make the right decision for the company because the company would have the ability to see that the suppliers and parts he was choosing were the best option.

If this all sounds too simple, that's because it is...to an extent. There are many more factors that go into making buying decisions than simply the cost of the part and making sure the supplier has enough inventory to meet demand. One persistent example over the past several years has been the country of origin and the potential risk factors associated with sourcing from that country. Companies must understand where their parts originate from, considering both spend and the number of parts. This knowledge is crucial for mitigating issues when natural disasters, tariffs, or other supply chain shocks occur in that region. Specifically, understanding tariffs can help companies anticipate and manage cost increases. More location data also reduces a company's risk exposure by enabling them to diversify their sourcing locations.

That's what LevaData does. We aggregate and then standardize all known data for commodities, restoring data integrity through consistent and automated review of your operational spend data. This means that companies can eventually create a system of record that works at the MPN level to identify all potential parts suppliers and their prices, enabling better-informed decision making.

Our data provides line of sight into part risk awareness by serving up risk attributes like lead times, Years to End of Life (YTEOL), age, and single source risk. We provide information on alternate parts (parts with the same form and functionality but different MPNs) to compare costs and key risk attributes. Our data includes location awareness for companies to know where their parts are manufactured so they can respond when there is a geographic shock in the world. We even have a tariff tool that allows users to input various tariff amounts for an idea of the impact it would have on their sourcing from certain regions.

What LevaData does, in essence, is allow companies to solve use cases that supply chain and company leaders care about. We're kind of like those *Choose Your Own Adventure* novels that were popular back in the 1980s and '90s, giving you a chance to test different sourcing possibilities to determine in advance what the probable outcome will be so that you don't end up in metaphorical quicksand or a pit of snakes. We're a decision engine that allows companies to run scenarios and make data-driven choices.

This is the evolution of decision intelligence and integration with AI. Within sixty days of onboarding with LevaData, companies gain valuable insights to make better, more informed sourcing decisions. In two months, you can have cost savings to fund future products before you even close out your quarterly financial statements. The possibilities are there, but people have to choose to change.

John Wooden, in his wizardly sports way, created his own kind of "system of record" to lead his team to unparalleled success. He had visibility into the strengths and weaknesses of each of his players and was aware of his competition as well. He used the data he had to create a culture of unity for his team, where everyone would make the best possible decisions for the team. Wooden knew that his approach couldn't be one-size-fits-all. With each new competitor he had to be able to make new decisions and test new theories, but still with the same vision of winning. It worked well.

Wooden famously said, "Failure is not fatal, but failure to change might be." Our mindset might push us toward short-term safety and comfort, but our inability to adapt to a changing landscape could also be setting us up for long-term struggle. Leaders need to be aware of their own biases and fears, particularly as they relate to data and technology. They need to aim higher through the coming decade, and the use of AI should be a part of that vision.

There is a change in the sourcing winds. Some companies will keep their eyes down, focusing on each leak that springs up and trying to patch it as quickly as they can until the next problem arises. In their efforts to stay afloat, they're losing sight of the changing environment around them. Rather than being a problem to fix, sourcing could become a company's competitive advantage. It could add wind to their sails through better decision making, cost savings, and reduced risk. But change won't happen unless someone is brave (or concerned) enough to make it happen.

SEVEN

Shark in the Water: Our Perception of Risk

I remember my first time seeing the movie *Jaws*, sometime in the early 1980s. Based on the book by Peter Benchley, the story was about an enormous, blood-thirsty, people-devouring shark that was loose in the waters of the fictitious town of Amity Island. Despite this killer lurking in the waters, the mayor of Amity Island gives the green light to the town's Fourth of July festivities. Why? Because he is concerned about losing tourist revenue. There is literally a gigantic shark slowly eating the town alive, but the mayor and other residents do not want to close the beaches and potentially lose out on selling ice cream and souvenir t-shirts until the situation is handled. Spoiler alert: there is terror at the beach and more people die. Not a great tourism selling point.

While the movie *Jaws* was a fictitious story of what happens when we're incorrectly evaluating risk, the real-life "Jaws Effect" had an impact on everything from decreased beach tourism to cruel and questionable shark-hunting practices from sports fishermen. People became terrified of sharks and the apparent risk they presented to human life, even though statistics pointed to the contrary. Most shark species are, in fact, not dangerous to humans, and the risk of a shark attack occurring is pretty rare. What should humans be more concerned about in open water? The water itself. Drowning, from rip currents, undertows, or lack of swimming skills, is the leading cause of water-related deaths. While you're keeping your eyes open for fins slicing through the water looking to turn you into their lunch, flesh-eating bacteria (*vibrio vulnificus*) actually poses a statistically greater risk to your health.

The goal of this story is to highlight that while we often know what risks are out there, our ability to prioritize them in order of true importance is heavily influenced by cognitive bias. We filter information based on our own personal experiences and preferences, often discarding data-driven facts in the process. As a result, we sometimes keep our eyes on the wrong risks because our brains tell us they're the most dangerous ones.

Supply chain risk is a challenging subject to write a chapter on when really there is enough to talk about that I could fill several books. There is so much to say and so many angles to take, from compliance risk to talent shortages and environmental risks. There are ESG pressures with an ever-changing goalpost for companies to try and reach. Cybersecurity and third-party supplier vulnerabilities become greater concerns as technology evolves and becomes more interconnected. When it comes to a manufacturing company's risk exposure, it makes sense that sourcing is an area of primary concern.

Every business wants to "de-risk" their supply chain and build a resilient system of production. Their methods of prioritizing and approach risk vary greatly, though. Many companies evaluate their sourcing risk by asking things like, "Did we get our parts and material on time?" or, "Did we get favorable payment terms?" Cost and lead time are, understandably, important potential risks to stay on top of. And because companies love metrics, they might create a scorecard to measure these risks and report on them. Companies send surveys to their suppliers to evaluate and attempt to quantify the relationship. This is what I call "umbrella risk." It's an attempt to gauge the overall health of the supply chain. It's basing this evaluation on the data points that seem to be within the greatest control of the procurement department.

Companies may also evaluate their sourcing "portfolio risk" based on the aggregation of where parts are coming from and how many (or few) suppliers are being utilized to produce a product. They may try to evaluate the health of their suppliers and identify if there are red flag warnings for concern. It's a bit of a feel-good exercise that can make procurement departments feel like they're doing something proactive, even though it's something that they have almost no control over at the end of the day.

For many companies, the prospect of portfolio risk is daunting, as they are already making the most informed decisions possible with the data at their disposal. Learning that their best option for price or lead time is also a risky option puts them in a difficult decision. The result is often to turn a blind eye to the risk, regardless of where it lands, because they still believe they're working with their best supplier options based on their own narrow view of risk. Sourcing teams often have constant feelings of underlying fear, uncertainty, and doubt that someday this risk might play out. Without the willingness or information to make a change, however, they sit and hope for the best, knowing that there may be a major supply chain shock in their future.

As I write this book, there is a new supply chain shock that has caught manufacturing off guard and resulted in major supply chain uncertainty: US tariffs on imported goods. Tariffs are nothing new to international trade and are often not challenging to manage as long as you know what the rates are and what materials or goods they apply to. Instead, our current tariff situation is rife with talk of what will be happening, only for the rates to be changed a few weeks later or paused for months. There are negotiations on what countries should and shouldn't be tariffed and what goods are considered necessary for US manufacturers and should be exempt.

The behemoth companies of the US are testing their political sway to see what exemptions they can negotiate with the government for themselves, while small- and medium-sized manufacturers feel an increased pressure to somehow adapt to ever-changing conditions that may have a material impact on their ability to source goods and sell products at a price that US consumers are willing to pay. It is an incredibly tumultuous time for sourcing professionals and the potential risk for businesses is high. Things get complicated quickly.

In these situations, companies need an agile way to run and test sourcing scenarios. They need the ability to say, "If the tariffs with China are 120 percent, then I will source this part from country X, Y, or Z instead." They need ways to analyze their current parts inventory to consider reusing a greater percentage of parts in their next product design rather than importing new parts, metals, ingredients, or materials. We have launched a tariff analyzer as part of our data analysis platform that companies can run, and re-run, and re-run again based on the latest tariff rates by country and product.

What we're currently seeing, however, is that companies have yet to shift their focus to sourcing future parts, metals, ingredients, and materials. That shock will come later. For now, their "hair on fire" risk seems to be how to price and move the current inventory they've already produced. They are heavily focused on selling their finished products and have not yet shifted their gaze toward how they will manage the next round of product development and production. When that time comes there will be a violent pendulum swing toward sourcing. It is going to hit hard, and companies will flip from finished good concern to subassemblies and components concern. The need to know all potential parts sourcing options will be greater than ever before and, unfortunately, the companies who do not plan for this in some way are likely going to be out of business unless government policies change. Those who are proactive in their sourcing departments have a greater ability to weather this unpredictable storm. Fear and emotional override are what will keep many sourcing departments from making a change.

Sourcing leaders need to reframe the way they look at risk. The reality of business risk is often quite different from whatever the present sourcing risk of the moment is. Risk is in part whatever is happening externally, but there is a hidden risk in how a company responds or doesn't respond to that risk. Risk may come from how a company prioritizes its concerns, particularly if human bias cannot differentiate the most significant risks from the most visible risks. We create risk by focusing on the present and how it impacts us, all while hoping the future will somehow sort itself out.

Business owner Elon Musk was famously quoted as saying, "There's a tremendous bias against taking risks. Everyone is trying to optimize their ass-covering." We must begin to assess our business risks from a fresh perspective and seek to understand the underlying reasons behind our decisions. When we make a choice, are we considering what the best option for the business is, or the option that is merely the safest, easiest to quantify? Additionally, it is crucial to determine whether our risk assessments offer only short-term security or if they will benefit us in the long run as well.

In the new agentic AI world of sourcing, the data allows you to make the best decisions for your organization. You no longer have to call Joe in Saskatchewan for your lead time because the system has the data. You don't have to hope your charming personality or company size will be your negotiating tools because you'll have a single source of information with all the available suppliers and pricing for the raw materials or parts you need. In fact, in many of these situations, you don't even have to figure out the "right decisions" because they are presented to you via the data. Your role is to choose the best outcome based on what matters most to the company, which often means price and lead times from suppliers. Agentic AI isn't meant to fully remove humans from the process, but it does help replace emotion-based decision making with data-backed decisions.

The perceived risk of having your supply chain disrupted because your one vendor in one part of the world experiences a shock is like panicking about the potential existence of a shark in the water without realizing that you're actually being pulled under by the current. LevaData's ability to contextualize a company's supply chain data and provide a single place to manage suppliers and contract manufacturers is incredibly powerful. If a supply chain shock happens, it becomes a frustration, but it's generally no longer debilitating to your business. You find the next best vendor to keep your production moving.

If it's as easy as knowing the other vendors that are out there, then why can't companies simply keep a spreadsheet of their vendor options? Because it's a nearly impossible process to handle manually. If you produce a product that requires a thousand different parts, the process of identifying potential vendors for each part and keeping their parts and pricing data up to date is not attainable nor efficient, particularly if the product design team is already in the process of designing the next model, which will have new parts requirements. What you need is a real data geek.

One of our clients is a multinational business technology company that was looking to de-risk their business model, though they weren't entirely sure what their real risks were. As tech innovators with nearly one hundred years of company history, they grew their business by acquiring many smaller companies along the way. Their company culture was one that valued the uniqueness and autonomy of what each acquisition brought to the table, and they allowed many of these organizations to continue operating as siloed entities. They let the experts continue doing what they were already successfully doing.

That approach can be great...to an extent. This company discovered that many of their departments were handling their own sourcing needs individually. The thought behind it was that they knew the parts and materials needed to produce their product and already had established relationships. With LevaData's platform and ability to aggregate and contextualize data into one single source of information, they discovered that many of their departments were buying the same parts and materials, even from the same vendors, but at very different costs!

This data intelligence gave them the opportunity to really save. If they could centralize their purchasing, they would have far more leverage with suppliers to negotiate better prices and terms. Doing so would offer a noticeable reduction to their cost of goods sold (COGS) and would streamline ordering and part reuse. This seemed like a slam-dunk for the company to reduce their exposure risk and increase their cost savings. Interestingly, they struggled to make the change.

LevaData's technology exposed risks hidden in their current sourcing model, but it also exposed another risk: the human risk. This multinational company was not sure that they could (or wanted to) change their culture and shift away from federated entities to a more cohesive organization. It didn't matter what the data showed. Even the best data intelligence in the world loses its value without action. This client saw the data, knew what they had to do, and still chose otherwise because they lacked a culture that expected and knew how to manage change. Instead, they opted for what felt like the safest compromise to address their sourcing risk while not rocking the emotional boat. They decided that 10 percent of their parts would be negotiated for the entire company. Using our data, they chose their most strategic parts that were either high-price, high-importance, or highly-purchased items.

Even when the data says, "You're making a risky decision," it is not always enough to overcome the human emotional element of change. If a team or company has the belief system that change is painful or that change may mean failure, it is harder to manage and mitigate risk. Our client didn't have the strongest change agent culture, but at least now they had the awareness and were awakened to the problems of their data. Whether they wanted to do something with the data or not was completely up to them. Some companies choose not to change until organizational duress demands change. When the risk of not changing is too great, companies turn back to us and our data.

LevaData is not a company of tech generalists. We are the geekiest geeks in our narrow slice of procurement, direct material sourcing. We were founded on the belief there is a better path for the sourcing profession, a path that includes the tools to understand disparate data and collaboratively make the best possible sourcing decisions for your organization in a factual way. LevaData's tools can't do much for you when it comes to sales or warehousing, but in the realm of direct material sourcing, we are unmatched.

Our true advantage is that we're one of the only technology tools available that has mapped the world of parts. We are the leaders in identifying Fit Form Function (FFF) alternative part options. This means not only identifying sourcing options for parts with the same parts number but also identifying equivalent parts that have the same fit, form, and function but with a different serial number. The result is often that companies identify more potential suppliers than they realized were available to them. This gives companies a greater ability to weigh what they want to spend and where they want to buy it from.

Mapping parts in the world of FFF is not easy for companies to do. As a third-party manager in sourcing, your suppliers are not going to share what their competitors' FFFs are. If you're a manufacturer that is managing relationships with over 600 suppliers to buy your company's 18,000 different part types, trying to uncover the FFF for each of those parts is an outright nightmare. But when you're buying hundreds of thousands to millions of parts each year, having this data matters. Visibility into FFF options is a key way to manage and mitigate your sourcing risk.

One LevaData client is a popular small appliance brand in the US. For many years they manufactured their own products before realizing that their true strength was in developing intellectual property, not the actual product manufacturing itself. Like many other companies out there, they switched to contract manufacturing. This meant negotiating and contracting with another company to build their products. Each time a new product came out, they had a new negotiation.

It didn't take them long to realize that they had no way to determine if they were getting a good deal or not. Without their own direct material sourcing department, they lacked the human bandwidth they once had to research and evaluate each product part. Instead, they could create a budget for what they hoped to spend on the products and then hope that the contract manufacturer would come back with a price that was within that budget. As movie director James Cameron once said while filming *Avatar*, "Hope is not a strategy."

Finding LevaData gave this company leverage. They now had a system of record to input the parts their products would need and the cost associated with them. Without this data, they had no way to know if they were getting a good deal from the contract manufacturers. Without this data, they had no leverage to say, "Actually, here is the cost range for that part."

In this client case, they reduced their sourcing risk by off-loading it to the contract manufacturer to figure out. At the same time, they took on a new risk—losing control of the BOM cost. Contextualized, accurate data is how they now manage and mitigate that risk. The control and decision-making power were back in their hands. They had the knowledge now to understand what the real risks, the real fears, should be.

When companies have part visibility inside their BOM, they can become more efficient with their part sourcing. They can focus on the real risks of raw material sourcing (the only two real risks in my opinion): lead time and price. The risk of a tsunami or geopolitical tensions are no longer major risks if you know all your options for sourcing parts and materials. Companies realize that it's okay to have all your eggs in one basket as long as you have control of what happens to that basket.

The manufacturing companies that benefit most from our data tools are the growth-oriented companies that care about cost and risk to their parts. The companies that build products. Scaling as a manufacturing company is serious business, and being able to receive parts and manage costs to meet an exploding customer demand is incredibly challenging. Often, these growing companies lack the human power to handle their sourcing needs and are faced with a decision: do they hire a lot of people, or do they support their current team with better technology and data?

LevaData doesn't give answers. We don't outright tell you, "Buy this, not that." What we do provide are data-driven insights for evaluating your sourcing options based on what matters most to your company. In addition to building data integrity, you now have location awareness, part risk awareness, saving opportunities, and alternate part options. You have visibility into what your options are and the ability to collaborate more effectively with your suppliers. We don't eliminate your risks, but we can show you what your risks actually are and ways to potentially mitigate them.

We can be less afraid of perceived risks when we open ourselves up to more accurate information. It took decades of shark reeducation to improve public perception of sharks and their real danger (or lack thereof). Just before his death in

2006, *Jaws* author Peter Benchley said, "I couldn't write *Jaws* today. The extensive new knowledge of sharks would make it impossible for me to create, in good conscience, a villain of the magnitude and malignity of the original." It's amazing what quality data can do!

SECTION 3

WE'RE
GOING TO NEED
A BETTER BOAT

EIGHT

A Deep Dive into the Data Gulch

Throughout this book I've mentioned how important it is to have the right tool for the job. I found that to be true in my home remodeling endeavors and in hand-shaping surfboards. I've found it in homebrewing beer, where proper sanitation and precise measurements are crucial to a quality output. To build on the last chapter about the movie *Jaws*, it makes me think of the movies famous line, "We're going to need a bigger boat!" They recognized that the tool they had was not sufficient to accomplish the task at hand. Because they couldn't get that bigger boat or better tools, however, they did the best they could with what they had and were ultimately victorious, though not without casualties in the process. The lesson is not that you need just the right tool to do work (there are a lot of ways to get a job done). The lesson is that we don't have to struggle and suffer as hard as we do to get jobs done if we have the option to choose better tools.

The supply chain market is full of large and popular software options. I'd be shocked if I ever met someone in the supply chain realm who wasn't familiar with SAP Ariba, Blue Yonder, Oracle, or Coupa. These programs are widely utilized and boast numerous impressive capabilities. They excel in fulfilling their primary purpose: seamlessly integrating various components of the supply chain to improve data visibility. Among their many features, they offer "business directories" that assist sourcing professionals in identifying a broader range of potential suppliers from an extensive vendor database. In essence, they appear to meet the diverse needs of supply chain professionals. But they do not.

If these leading software vendors really could do it all, though, then why do sourcing departments still experience major decision-making challenges? Why does working in sourcing still frequently feel like everyone's running around with their hair on fire, trying to anticipate or resolve the next procurement shock? If you have identified that there are still significant risks or challenges to your sourcing process, then it means that the tools you have are not sufficient for the job at hand. You and your team or company may be facing unnecessary hardship, not because you've chosen the wrong tool, but because the tool just isn't the best one for the job you're trying to do or the problem you're trying to fix. The boat in *Jaws* wasn't necessarily a bad boat; it just wasn't the best boat to take on a creature of that size.

Many of today's cloud-based P2P software solutions are akin to traveling on a large, secure ship with only a small porthole to peer through. While you can glimpse the water and perhaps discern your direction or past journey, you miss out on a vast expanse of insights. You are aware of their existence, yet your current view does not provide the comprehensive visibility you need. So what do you do? Do you continue to rely on the limited perspective because it is "good enough" and conveniently accessible? Or do you choose to make a change and embrace a solution that offers the full spectrum of visibility you deserve?

I faced my own lesson of why it pays to do things the right way versus the convenient way one time while I was building a sailboat. Yes, me...the guy from Wisconsin with the can-do attitude that earns me the occasional eyeroll from friends and family members, decided to restore a cheap, old sailboat to its full glory. Some may have considered this a fool's mission, particularly given the fact that I had never actually been on a sailboat until I was in my mid-twenties and I had almost zero knowledge about how to sail one. But if there is one thing you should know about me, it's that I am perpetually curious and wildly optimistic. My love of figuring things out took over. With the growth mindset phrase that had been slathered on my children throughout their education, I told myself that I simply didn't have the know-how...*yet*!

For the next two years I spent most of my free moments, mostly on weekends and breaks over the summer, learning how to strip and reseal teak, lay fiberglass, update plumbing and rewire electrical, install interior walls, and replace all the running and standing rigging. My primary lesson learned was that there are numerous ways to complete a task. Of those ways, some are efficient and some are inefficient. Sometimes my mind would take the path of inefficiency, not because I wanted to make life harder on myself, but because I was falling into old, comfortable habits, even in this new endeavor. For example, when it came to removing and refinishing the teak wood from the sailboat, I started carefully hand-sanding each piece. Hand-sanding had always worked for me on my smaller projects, so when I was presented with something to sand, my brain said, "Keith, go grab the sandpaper!"

It didn't take long for me to look at the large stack of teak pieces waiting to be refinished for me to realize that this was not the best path forward. I paused and considered other ways to go about the task—the most obvious one being to get an electric orbital sander. What should have been an easy aha moment didn't exactly feel that way. This new path felt disruptive to my work. It was annoying to use some of my available work time on driving to The Home Depot. I was a bit grumpy about investing additional money on this project to buy the sander. (I know, I know. They're only like $50!) In hindsight, I was glad I changed my direction when I did. The orbital sander ended up saving me a tremendous amount of time and physical pain on the job. I learned a valuable lesson by pausing, determining a better way, and choosing a new course forward.

Deciding to work efficiently, particularly when we're already in a workflow, doesn't happen easily. It takes time to determine what our possible pathways are and then weigh our options to move forward with the best one. New pathways often create new barriers of resistance. There may be a fear of learning something new or trying something untested, even if others have done it before with great success or the reviews on the product are fantastic. Fear acts like a constrictor to our mind's pathways. When we're operating from a place of fear, we can rarely see all the options available to us, and we lack the creative bandwidth to explore new possibilities.

I have always admired people who are fearless. I love meeting people who have the intelligence to know what they want, balanced with the determination to actually pursue it. I strive to be both fearlessly naive and hopelessly optimistic. That was the story of my sailboat experience. Perhaps if I had actually thought through everything that would go into redoing that boat, I never would have bought it in the first place. Instead, I was gifted an incredibly rewarding experience and many happy memories with my wife and friends on our sailing trips. At this point in my life now, I've owned several boats...though I no longer have the desire to restore them. I'm glad that I went for it and continue to surround myself with other curious people who are comfortable with the meandering path if it means finding the right way.

LevaData operates with a unique approach, distinct from simply following established paths or solving already well-addressed issues. Our technology tools are not designed to replace major platforms like SAP Ariba, Oracle, or Coupa. Instead, we aim to be a highly specialized tool within the fleets of manufacturing companies. We serve as the vehicle to navigate the vast ocean of external manufacturing data, making sense of years of accumulated internal data and utilizing them together to make the best data-driven decisions.

This is not a magical solution where you need to close your eyes and hope it works. We have years of client success stories that attest to this innovative approach to direct material sourcing. Our system helps you escape from the chaos of spreadsheets and create a single source of truth for your sourcing needs.

Our process begins with foundational actions to improve the quality and usability of data, a goal every company should strive to achieve. The issue of data asymmetry is prevalent among medium-sized businesses and almost unavoidable in larger corporations. Each team or department maintains its own system of record or data repository, leading to siloed information that is not shared across the organization. This results in an asymmetric data problem, where departments draw different conclusions based on the limited information available to them. Over time, this accumulation of disparate data forms what we call the Data Gulch.

We initiate our data contextualization efforts by loading the operational sourcing spend into LevaData. It's easy for us to load the parts, metals, and ingredients that our customers need for producing their product, and we do it at scale, often loading millions and billions of spend at once. This is the foundation. While much of the supply chain is focused on forecasting (supply chain planning), minimizing cost (finance), and delivering new products (engineering leadership), we are focused on the data story in front of the customer.

We integrate all this data into a unified view that sourcing professionals can use to make informed purchasing decisions and share with other departments. Think of us as a sophisticated data blender, where each team contributes their ingredients—some of which may not initially seem to fit together. LevaData processes this information and blends it into data sets that provide new insights. By incorporating both a company's internal data and our access to global market data sets, we have developed a recipe that works. The result is a wealth of data presented in a new way to create real insights, alternatives, options, and scenarios with a focus on continuous parts optimization.

We achieve this by contextualizing billions of data points. Think about that. This is akin to having a data point on every single person in the United States and being able to filter it to create the perfect team for your company based on the skill sets and experience that matter most to you. It is remarkable to have access to such vast amounts of data and be able to use it meaningfully, yet this is precisely what we have specialized in. We do this at the manufacturing parts level, enabling you to make decisions based on a broad field of data.

LevaData customers, on average, have an annual direct material spend of over $1 billion. That is a tremendous amount of purchase transactions. Our customers generally experience a 90 percent increase in insight visibility of all parts that drive cost optimization and sourcing resiliency. That narrow window in the boat just widened tremendously, and now all those transactions comprising the $1 billion can be viewed through an optimized lens. We do this by leveraging data at the product and commodity levels, utilizing multiple data storage locations and formats. We also integrate company data with other external sources of data, some that your company likely does not have access to yet.

We work differently because our system is not a framework

to hold data; it's not another type of data lake, data mesh, or warehouse. LevaData's tools are AI decision engines that continuously take insightful data and prioritize it to direct user action. With this information, companies can quickly pivot and begin to buy smarter. Understanding how we work, though, can still feel a bit esoteric. It's complex technology and there isn't much out there to compare it to. We don't sell to our potential customers. Instead, we show you your sourcing spend directly in our application.

The only way to know if this is going to work for your business is to try it. Companies can give us a subset of their data and within one week we will contextualize it with our market data to provide decision intelligence. We do it at scale and we do it for free because we have complete and total confidence in our tech capabilities. We know that our system is a game-changer for sourcing departments. Decide what data you want to go into the system and see the results for yourself. There are multiple ways in which our data systems can support and strategize sourcing decisions for greater resilience.

One of my favorite client stories is of a US-based company that experienced hypergrowth over the past several years. They are currently one of the world's largest companies when ranked by market capitalization. When they came to us, they had an incredibly complex supply chain for their tech manufacturing business and their sourcing was done entirely by a team overseas. That team worked off spreadsheet data to track and compare component pricing through original design manufacturers (ODMs) and contract manufacturers (CMs). Our first step was to contextualize their spreadsheet data, plus our additional market data, into a single source of truth. Through this process alone they were able to clearly identify better buying decisions and quickly recognize cost savings on their BOM.

Given the initial success with our technology, they wanted to know what else could be done. We're not just a company of data intelligence for buying decisions; we also facilitate the sharing of information and the negotiation process. This company started to use our Request for X (RFX) programs, whether they were requesting proposals or fulfilling requests for information from customers. During COVID, the RFX programs became particularly useful in identifying and sharing information around the country of origin of their sourced parts. The cost of transporting goods during COVID spiked, making location a priority consideration in manufacturing.

At the time of this writing, in 2025, the global manufacturing market is once again taking a keen interest in where parts are located due to the threat of cost-prohibitive tariffs on goods imported from certain countries. This client is not only leaning heavily on our location data, which factors in the impact of proposed and enacted tariff rates, but they are also sharing their findings and automated forecasts with their supply partners to support them in managing these geopolitical shockwaves. Their story highlights the ability to both save money and become more efficient in the role of sourcing.

Another client of ours is a Japanese-based manufacturer that was utilizing a sophisticated system to alert them to risks to their supply chain. If there was a weather event that might impact one of their suppliers, or governmental instability, or new legislation, they received notice to take action. It's a great tool, except that it did nothing to support them in determining *what* action to take. They came to LevaData for greater part level alternative options and pricing visibility. With our system they could now explore alternative options, locations, and prices, allowing them to de-risk and take action whenever they received an alert.

Due to this improved decision-making ability, they utilized our tools to de-risk other areas of their sourcing related to end-of-life parts. End-of-life parts are those that are no longer manufactured. They can become especially dangerous as a manufacturer because it may force a company to re-engineer products to continue production. Through blending and contextualizing the data on their thousands of part components, they were able to identify that over one third of their current parts were considered end-of-life. That was an eye-opening moment. With the data provided, they were able to identify all available sources of where to continue buying the parts they needed while also strategizing with their product design teams to create new iterations of their popular products using more readily-available components.

Not all our clients handle their manufacturing themselves. One well-known vehicle manufacturer collaborates with many of their suppliers on sub-assembly components. This means that a supplier will source multiple parts and produce a piece of the vehicle, such as a wire harness. Before coming to LevaData, this vehicle manufacturer could only leverage its size and buying power to negotiate on price. They didn't have any visibility into the actual cost of the parts to make their vehicle components, nor did they know what a reasonable lead time would be.

The LevaData application was able to give the vehicle manufacturer insight into what the vehicle component *could* potentially cost if the sub-assembly supplier sourced the best part options. This allowed the vehicle manufacturer to determine if they were paying a fair price for their components. They also had new insights around the expected lead times to receive those individual parts. This knowledge gave them more leverage in negotiating how long the sub-assembly supplier could take to produce the components. Their data drove new conversations that this manufacturer would not have had without visibility into their data.

Once the risks around cost and time were addressed, the vehicle manufacturer looked for other ways to improve the resilience of their supply chain. They realized that a fair number of their product components were single-source parts, meaning there was only one manufacturer that made that one part. While it's very bespoke to design and sell one-of-a-kind products, it's also an incredible threat to production and sales should anything, and I mean *anything*, happen to that supplier. Utilizing a custom muffler produced by a specific artisan in Wisconsin can enhance the uniqueness and exclusivity of your vehicle. However, if this artisan becomes unavailable due to illness, injury, or other personal pursuits, it could lead to significant sourcing challenges and increased costs. Our application empowered the sourcing team to identify all their single-source

CONQUERING THE DECISION ABYSS

components so that they could, at the very least, shift to a dual-sourced component. Still bespoke products, but with significantly less risk.

With each client we serve, the process starts simply: identify alternate options, buy smarter, save money. That is just the tip of the sourcing efficiency iceberg, though. Having data visibility means exploring, identifying, and mitigating other forms of sourcing risk and discovering new means of operating efficiently. Even with this knowledge and these abilities, there are still companies that do not move forward. They become paralyzed by the thought of taking a different path forward. They grip their trusty sandpaper, even after knowing that an orbital sander is an option.

They start with numerous reasons and excuses for why their system is broken. They try to rationalize why they're okay with that. The thought of turning over sample data to learn what is possible gets clouded by the fears of "What data should I even provide?" and the shame of "I don't want to be judged for the way I'm currently doing things." The unfortunate reality is that some people face fear, and fear wins. Resistance to change, reliance on legacy systems, high implementation costs, and data fragmentation become barriers to improvement.

Sourcing can be like trying to solve a Rubik's Cube. You can get one side right, but the other five faces may be off. Some companies stop on one side, content with their successful completion of a small piece. Others keep trying the same moves over and over again, hoping to solve the puzzle. We've all heard the childhood rhyme "If at first you don't succeed, try, try again." That mindset and approach to new or challenging tasks worked great in our youth, helping us learn foundational skills.

As we grew and our lives became more complex, however, many of us have come to learn that this repetitive approach to problem solving no longer serves us. In fact, in a quote that is often misattributed to Albert Einstein and is likely from author Rita Mae Brown, we have learned that "the definition of insanity is doing the same thing over and over again and expecting different results." Instead, the problem of the Data Gulch is better addressed with the mindset of a Navy SEAL.

The Navy SEALs, an elite United States Navy special operations force, approach problem solving for their highly complex missions with the mindset of "find a new way." They are known for their adaptability and willingness to find unconventional solutions in challenging situations. They are also known for their resilience. Finding a new way means exploring the tools and resources available to solve the problem you face. Sometimes, it means breaking away from the conventional or mainstream. Rather than the pessimistic mindset of "this is how things have always been done," the Navy SEALs operate with a grit mindset that includes hope-led cognition, the belief that goals can be achieved by discovering the right pathway forward. We do not need to opt in to our own suffering in business or in life.

LevaData follows this Navy SEALs mindset. We knew there had to be a better way, and we followed our passion, interest, skillset, and all-around geekery to solve the problem of the Data Gulch and the Decision Abyss. We set the goal of improving operational efficiency for companies by optimizing spending and sourcing resilience at the parts level. Our pathway to this goal included developing a common operational language between disparate data sources so that business leaders and teams could make informed decisions. We widened the ship's porthole to provide unmatched visibility into how parts and materials can be optimally sourced to create the desired finished goods. We found ways to provide more accurate matching between what companies can produce and what they should be producing.

We offer solutions that can help companies overcome these barriers and embrace change effectively. Clear communication and training, cost-effective solutions, and rapid ROI delivery are key strategies that LevaData employs to facilitate the adoption of new technologies. Change drives progress. In the context of supply chains, adopting new technologies and methodologies can lead to significant improvements in efficiency, cost savings, and resilience. For instance, integrating advanced analytics and AI can enhance decision making, optimize inventory management, and improve demand forecasting. Companies that embrace change are better positioned to adapt to market fluctuations, regulatory changes, and unexpected disruptions. While LevaData may not be the biggest boat on the sea, we are the right one for this job.

NINE

A NEED FOR SPEED

When Apple was founded back in 1976 with Steve Jobs and Steve Wozniak tinkering in a California garage, the focus was not on the aesthetics of their motherboard but the ease of use. At the time, companies like Commodore and IBM were leading in the computer market, but their motherboards had to be assembled by technology-savvy consumers. Jobs and Wozniak looked at the problem and decided to work differently, with Wozniak originally hand-assembling each of the units that they sold. Their marketing pitch was "Why waste time building a computer?"

A large part of Apple's success has been due, in part, to its focus on identifying the most acute pain points of its customers and addressing them effectively. While some tech geeks may have loved the process of building their own motherboards, even more people wanted a microcomputer that was constructed correctly and could start working immediately. Steve Jobs said, "You have got to start with the customer experience and work back to the technology. You can't start with the technology and figure out how you're going to sell it." This mindset and approach were integral to Apple's early success and proved immensely profitable as a business strategy.

Apple broadened their customer base simply by making their products a bit more accessible and easier to use than the competition. They understood that excellent design started with the customer experience of their product. This simple difference in how they worked allowed them to take on the tech giants of their time and gain market share.

There is another key lesson that leaders can take from Apple. Great leaders do not need to understand every technical detail to be incredibly effective in their work. Jobs was a psychology and philosophy student in college before he dropped out. He later went on to study things like art and Zen Buddhism. He, nor any other Apple CEO to date, had a background in computer science or years of experience in coding. Jobs was a visionary who wasn't afraid to break from the cultural norms to do what he felt was the right thing for the company or consumer. In the year before he took on a financial leadership role, Apple lost more than $1 billion. The following year, he led them to profits of $309 million. Keeping his eye on the end user paid off!

Apple's current CEO, Tim Cook, took the company to a market capitalization of over $3 trillion. If Apple were its own country, it would rank in the top ten largest economies, ahead of Italy, Brazil, Russia, and Canada. What is Cook's degree in? Industrial engineering. His mind works in a way that has allowed him to excel at supply chain management. Cook is known for keeping a tight control over his inventory and having a keen eye for cost savings opportunities. He thinks in terms of logistics, keeping the creation and flow of products moving in even more efficient ways.

It doesn't matter how well Tim Cook understands the computer coding behind each of Apple's products. He has some of the best people in the industry to handle that. What truly matters is that he remains dedicated to efficiently obtaining what he needs and delivering it to consumers swiftly, at the optimal price, and without compromising quality.

When LevaData was established, it was built with a steadfast commitment to our customers—sourcing professionals. From the outset, we recognized the unique challenges faced by sourcing departments, often operating with limited resources. We observed that while smooth operations occasionally garnered praise, any disruptions quickly led to scrutiny. Questions like "Why didn't the products get built on time?," "Why wasn't the quantity of parts sufficient?," "Why did material costs increase?," and "Why are our cost-of-goods increasing?" were all too common. Our mission has always been to support these professionals in overcoming such hurdles with efficiency and precision.

In my experience, the field of sourcing attracts incredibly diverse and interesting people. They're often very bright and adept at anticipating and solving problems before they happen. They can be heads-down, get-it-done type of people, but when they come up for air, they are also fun to be around and often have a quick-witted sense of humor. (Perhaps a strong sense of levity is necessary for the job.) Sourcing professionals don't need to be recognized as heroes, but they appreciate it when their efforts are noticed. In a curious observation, I've also noticed that those who survive in the demanding environment of sourcing for many years often have hobbies that would feel demanding or extreme, like distance running, exotic travel, or highly-specialized hobbies.

Those who dedicate their careers to sourcing excel at securing the best for everyone else yet often struggle to prioritize their own needs. As cost-conscious and skilled negotiators, it's understandable why they might resist changing systems that have served them well for years. Why add to an already heavy workload? Why learn something new when time is already scarce?

When we designed our system at LevaData, we kept the needs of sourcing professionals at the forefront. We knew they would need an enterprise sourcing application that could handle complicated and large data sets, but with the data presented in an understandable and usable format that wouldn't take extensive training to figure out. We knew they would need the flexibility to run different use case scenarios to weigh both the tangible and intangible benefits of selecting certain suppliers or geographic regions. We understood that some of the greatest stressors to their work were supply chain disruptions and finding alternate sources of parts, metals, ingredients, and materials. The ability to identify cost savings, even the smallest amounts, would be crucial to meeting their quarterly and annual financial goals.

Sourcing professionals require and merit enterprise applications that support their specific objectives around the clock. They also need to be able to share their findings across teams, departments, or with outside vendors in a way that is understandable for everyone. They need a system that delivers a clear ROI to substantiate the investments. And they don't have years to wait to see if the program was worth it. That is why LevaData doesn't make its customers wait. In fact, they can experience a trial run of the platform before they sign on with us to see the results for themselves.

LevaData has always focused on a narrow slice of the supply chain workflow because we wanted to become the best at one thing: direct material sourcing. We're fanatical about delivering excellence for our customers. While most companies might manage to contextualize data from a limited number of sources, we have mastered the integration of insights from a vast array of distinct data sets. Each unique source enriches the broader sourcing landscape, contributing invaluable perspectives to the comprehensive picture we provide. We go live with our clients' results after only sixty days, providing them real insights to make decisions on and begin saving money to fund future projects. It's not hyperbole to say we dominate at what we do. There is no leap of faith needed. You'll know if our system is for you.

One of my favorite client stories comes from a consumer electronics company with over $3 billion in annual revenue. For the sake of this story and their anonymity, we'll call them Rocket Corp. For many years, Rocket Corp. manufactured their own products and did pretty well for themselves. Over time, the cost of manufacturing rose to a point where Rocket Corp.'s products would potentially price themselves outside of what many of their customers would be willing to pay. They realized that their real strength was in the development of intellectual property and not the actual manufacturing itself. Rocket Corp. transitioned to contract manufacturing with the aspiration of reducing costs and maintaining stable prices for their finished goods, ensuring affordability for their customers.

Rocket Corp. had two major concerns when they made the switch from in-house manufacturing to contract manufacturing for their products. First, they needed a way to save on BOM costs while working with a contract manufacturer. Second, they needed to maintain the high quality of their product that their brand had become synonymous with. The challenge was that these two concerns were at odds with each other. How do you make the request to your contract manufacturers to bring down the cost of material inputs without sacrificing the more expensive components needed to maintain your status as a premium product? Rocket Corp. needed a unique solution for their contract manufacturing relationship to work.

Even though manufacturing was no longer under their control, Rocket Corp. had to ensure that their products performed to the same high standard that was synonymous with their brand. They performed a parts analysis and discovered that around 30 percent of the parts in one of their most popular products were considered strategic parts. These strategic parts were the ones that ultimately contributed to the quality of the product, while the other 70 percent had a less important role. Rocket Corp. created an agreement with their contract manufacturer that they would retain control of where those strategic parts were sourced. This would not be an area where the contract manufacturer could compromise quality by opting for cheaper inputs.

For the 70 percent non-strategic parts, however, Rocket Corp. gave their contract manufacturer the control in sourcing parts—to an extent. Rocket Corp. had a brilliant phrase that they used as a guidepost: "Trust, but verify." To them, "trust" meant that they should work as if their contract manufacturer had the best intentions and was ethically pricing and producing the product. "Verify" meant doing the due diligence to ensure that the pricing and timeframe for delivery were appropriate and reasonable. This is where Rocket Corp. needed LevaData.

The LevaData application allowed Rocket Corp. visibility into what it took to produce each of their products. They could see what each of their part options were, where the parts came from, and how long the lead times were. This information allowed them to create their own models for what it should cost and how long it should take to manufacture the product. These two pieces of information, cost and time, gave the company more negotiating leverage with their contract manufacturer.

There was a benefit to the contract manufacturer as well, though. Rocket Corp. could now point their contract manufacturer to new parts suppliers who could provide materials at a lower cost or with a shorter lead time. This data not only helped the company to get a better rate, but it also helped the contract manufacturer to identify better sourcing options at no additional cost to themselves. It was a win-win situation that strengthened the relationship between the two companies. And thanks to their "Trust, but verify" approach, Rocket

Corp. could refocus on their innovative product designs knowing that their contract manufacturer would produce quality goods, at a fair price, and in a reasonable period of time. This accelerated their product lifecycle and ability to be successful with new product introduction.

That wasn't the end for Rocket Corp. They understood the power of having data at their fingertips. This power comes not from the existence of data, but from contextualizing the data to serve up insights and turn them into action. Data is only valuable if you can do something with it. With LevaData's system, Rocket Corp. got curious about how else they could use their contextualized data to further streamline and economize their inventory levels now that they had sped up their production.

They began to explore what many manufacturers struggle with: part reuse. Part reuse is the percentage of old parts from previous products that can be used in new products. While companies need to continue to innovate, part reuse presents a very real problem for several reasons. Without proper management of parts, it can leave companies stuck with inventories of old, obsolete parts. Additionally, sourcing new parts is often more expensive, requiring both time and manual effort to perform due diligence on the supplier and negotiate a contract.

Given these issues it would seem like every company would be laser-focused on designing the next iteration of their products with as much part reuse as possible. It seems to make sense, yet many companies have an issue with old parts piling up or getting thrown away. Why wouldn't a company want to reuse old parts instead of letting them go to waste?

This is where having siloed data comes in. Part reuse (or lack thereof) matters to the sourcing team because it may add to their workload of finding new suppliers and negotiating new products. Part reuse matters to the warehousing team because they need to figure out what to do with the old inventory. Part reuse matters to the finance and sales teams who want to keep costs down but still provide innovative solutions. Part reuse matters to supply planners who may not be aware that existing inventory of parts can be used in other products.

The one team where part reuse doesn't generally seem to be the focus is the product design engineers. It's not that they don't care (they often don't have the same information as the other teams downstream). Their main focus is to continue to innovate with each iteration of a product to better meet consumers' needs while being conscious of cost. It's like they're looking through a small porthole, though, and are not focused on the same things that other teams are. As a result, part reuse might become everyone else's problem. Companies lack a concise way for all teams to understand the importance of project lifecycle management.

I don't want to make it sound like LevaData swoops in and suddenly teams are collaborating like never before, but it is possible. It's an aspirational place that we believe can be achieved through data sharing from a single source of truth. Imagine if, when it came time to design a product, the product design engineers had clear visibility into what parts inventory was already on hand and in what quantities. It would lessen the time wasted from having to rework designs due to new parts not being available in the right quantity, at the right time, or at the right price. The parts are already on hand; they just need to be reused.

When it comes to modern manufacturing, there is an absolute need for speed. The competition for parts, metals, ingredients, and other material continues to heat up, while the tastes of consumers shift faster than ever before. Meanwhile, threats of tariffs and poor parts management are causing companies to pump the brakes when it comes to innovating. In this time of conflicting needs, it's imperative to know your options. A solution to the modern manufacturing challenges is possible, but it requires a shift in mindset and the way things are done. Rocket Corp. had to face this shift first when they moved to contract manufacturing, then with how they engaged with their contract manufacturer. Finally, they had to shift in how they designed, making part reuse a priority right from the beginning of product development.

LevaData is not the panacea for all sourcing woes, but it is a powerful step in taking back control and remaining competitive in the manufacturing landscape. We're a tool that levels the playing field for the small guy against the big behemoth. We're an equalizer when it comes to going against larger incumbents. When it comes to developing your next strategy to survive and thrive in the business ecosystem, we are here to be your partners. Our success is rooted in your success.

That's why we are so committed to providing technology that can move the needle when it comes to making the right decisions in sourcing. We have felt the pain of our customers. We have listened to their concerns and fears. We know that time and evidence matter to them, which is why we've committed ourselves to delivering real insights within the same financial quarter. Like the founding Steves of Apple, we're not afraid to do things differently, because right now the sourcing industry needs something different and there isn't time to waste.

TEN

HEROES OF THE SUPPLY CHAIN

My parents raised me to look for the helpers (or perhaps I just internalized the wise words of Fred Rogers from the show *Mr. Rogers' Neighborhood*). Either way, I have learned from a young age that struggle is an inevitable part of life, but we don't have to go through it alone. Maybe that's why I have a special affinity for the underdog. In some ways, I feel like I have always sought them out and drawn inspiration from successful underdogs. Some of the movies that inspired me most were stories like *Rudy*, about a boy's seemingly impossible dream to play football for Notre Dame, and *Miracle*, based on the story of the 1980 United States Olympic hockey team and their journey defeating the Soviet Union and winning the gold medal. I love the company of those who recognize reality and insist on taking action to improve it.

Underdogs always seem to embody the qualities I admire and have desired to emulate: courage, adaptability, and resilience. Some of my favorite books are about the qualities or experiences of the underdog, like Angela Duckworth's book *Grit*. It is a treasure trove of stories and scientific examples of why some people persevere through difficulty while others fold. Duckworth defines grit as the "combination of passion and perseverance for a singularly important goal." Grit is different from intelligence and it's not due to luck or talent. There are plenty of talented people in this world who don't succeed because they lack the grit to do so. Underdogs are gritty people. They remind us that the system isn't always fair, but that people who refuse to quit—who fight despite the odds—can still succeed.

Maybe I seek out the underdog because I personally relate to them. I know what it's like to take on feats that seem impossible, unrealistic, or downright crazy. (Based on my early conversations with my wife, Bryn, writing this book may have been one of them.) I've always wanted to believe that life can be better and that I can take a proactive role in making it that way. I wanted to be the helper that others needed, seeking out those who seem underserved or neglected. I am drawn to others who have achieved success because of their hard work, ingenuity, and refusal to give up. Maybe it's why my desire to help people who work in sourcing is so strong. They are some of the hardest-working and determined people I know. For me, it goes beyond business. It's like a kinship.

The global procurement market is almost an $8 billion market in 2025. In a world dependent on global trade, procurement is fundamental to our existence. The efforts of sourcing professionals are vital to both our economy and daily lives. Yet somehow Hallmark has not created a selection of "Celebrate Your Sourcing Professionals Day" cards. I don't think most people realize how critical the role of sourcing is to the clothes they wear, the products they use, or the vehicles they drive. I don't know if most companies realize how critical the role of sourcing is. Somehow, even after COVID, sourcing gets overlooked.

Even within private equity, it's uncommon for investment dollars to flow directly towards sourcing technology. Instead, there's significant investment in areas like supply chain planning, warehousing, transportation, digital commerce, and inventory management systems. This focus is understandable. Traditional supply chain applications that have a direct impact on the P&L or customer experience have historically received more attention.

What about the solutions that target upstream procurement, like S2C? We know that supply chain disruptions are a reality for companies that make products. These disruptions are inevitable, and we can seldom predict their nature or timing. It's akin to residents of Florida, who face the annual threat of hurricanes yet often delay preparations until the storm is imminent, leading to a rush on grocery stores and gas stations. Why do we wait for disaster to strike before acting? Why do we only invest in necessary solutions when they're our last resort?

Sourcing is a critical component in the pursuit of resiliency of a supply chain. Effective sourcing strategies ensure that businesses can secure the best parts and materials and at optimal prices, maintain strong supplier relationships, and mitigate risks as they occur. Companies that focus on strong S2P processes have enhanced visibility and efficiency in creating purchase orders, invoicing, spend analysis, and supplier performance evaluation. Investing in these solutions proactively can mitigate the impact of unforeseen supply chain shocks and ensure smoother operations. By prioritizing sourcing, companies can build a resilient supply chain that is better equipped to handle disruptions and maintain continuity.

Psychologists have their thoughts on why we as individuals or business leaders avoid taking necessary, proactive steps for inevitable issues. For some people, it's a stress management response known as avoidance coping. Avoidance coping is when we ignore issues because it is easier in the short-term to avoid them instead of dealing with them. The result, however, is that problems often become harder to address once you're in them. Sourcing issues that are avoided often become more complex, requiring significantly more resources and effort to resolve.

Perfectionism may be another factor at play. I've mentioned before that many sourcing professionals are intelligent, talented, gritty people. They are accustomed to being successful at what they do. For the portion of them who fit the perfectionist personality type, identifying and acknowledging problems can be a real struggle. Instead, perfectionists often resort to procrastination, delaying the tasks that they assume they may not perform as successfully. They may hope that the challenge of the Data Gulch will somehow resolve itself without their intervention. Maintaining the illusion of perfection sometimes forces them to mentally bypass some very real issues they face.

Guilt, shame, and fear of conflict also create barriers to sourcing teams getting what they need. It's not that sourcing people don't know what's wrong. It's not that sourcing people don't deal with the challenges of the Decision Abyss on a daily basis. But if they are ignoring the issues or trying to overcome them through sheer grit and determination, it can lead to feelings of guilt or shame in admitting there is a problem that they need help with. These emotions are strong motivators in keeping their issues to themselves, not complaining, and avoiding potential conflict or rejection from company leadership that may think differently.

Perhaps private investors resist investing in sourcing technology because they don't understand what the issues are. I doubt that is the case, though. My hunch is that they do understand the issues. In fact, they know *exactly* how complex sourcing and S2C work is. For that reason, they choose to invest elsewhere in programs where the issues are more straightforward, and the benefits are often faster to be realized. Warehouse management feels like a reasonably-sized wave to overcome. Sourcing feels like a tsunami-sized investment risk.

When I evaluate the segments of the supply chain to identify where true value and significant opportunities lie, I am baffled to discover that the answer is clearly the sourcing workflow. Sure, you need good product design and an organized system to store things and fulfill orders...but if you don't have the right parts at the right time and the right cost, the other pieces don't matter as much. What good is the perfect design if you cannot find a source for several of the parts? The organization of your warehouse won't amount to much if you can't complete the assembly of your products because components were delayed due to a cyclone in the Pacific. And you can build and try to sell the most innovative product the world has ever seen, but if the cost of the components is so high that most consumers can't afford it, then few will get to experience the thrill of that innovation, and your inventory will collect dust.

When manufacturers invest in sourcing technology, it just makes sense. There is so much value to be gained and so many costs to be avoided. Smart sourcing technology solutions can provide manufacturing companies with better predictability on when they'll receive parts to manage the flow of assembly. Sourcing technology can facilitate better cash management not only by providing a broader lens to evaluate supplier options and alternative parts and costs, but also by improving efficiency in transactions. Companies with visibility into the cost and timing of their sourced parts can plan their spending more accurately.

Perhaps even more importantly, investing in the right sourcing technology means being proactive about supply chain risk. It means having the knowledge that a supply chain shock will inevitably strike at some point while also knowing in advance what other potential courses of action are to respond to the shock. This is what will be the greatest differentiator between those manufacturing companies who survive in the new sourcing environment and those who can't recover. When approximately 75–80 percent of your supply chain value is in the sourcing workflow, it is too risky not to be proactive about risk. Those who modernize their sourcing technology to keep up with the highly competitive world economy will gain a strategic advantage over the competition.

Some of my favorite client stories come from companies that could be considered the underdogs of their industries. They're the David and Goliath-type stories of the small guy using the right tool to compete against the giant. These LevaData customers were experiencing growth in their industries thanks to their innovative value propositions and their strong focus on strategic spending. In nearly all their stories, they understood the value of data—not simply having data but knowing how to use it. They excelled in their marketing because they used data to determine how to narrowly target their ideal customers. They excelled in their sales because they knew how to use a CRM to make contact and follow up at the most meaningful junctions in the customer relationship. They came to LevaData to excel in their supply chain by specifically targeting the area with the biggest value proposition: sourcing.

One of these clients is in the EV charging industry. You may have heard of the Goliath they're up against: a company called Tesla. While even entering the EV market may seem like a fool's quest when you have such a dominant industry leader, our client has already discovered ways to capitalize on their strengths and Tesla's shortcomings. Tesla's charging stations are expensive. For a long time, they could afford to be, positioning themselves as the luxury brand in the automotive industry. Tesla did a lot of the heavy lifting when it came to building consumer awareness about electric vehicles and changing consumer behaviors around charging stations.

Once more electric and hybrid vehicles entered the market and more consumers had the ability to afford going electric, our clients saw an opportunity to offer more affordable charging station options. To do this, though, they needed to be incredibly lean and efficient in their operations. Every dollar mattered to them and became an integral part of their philosophy. Their strategy worked and they began to gain market share in a way that most people wouldn't think was possible.

This EV charging company, however, experienced what all worthwhile companies experience with rapid growth. They needed to scale quickly and carefully. Rather than double the size of their sourcing team, they chose to source smarter. This is where we came in. Through using LevaData's AI technology, the company was able to keep their team size small yet supported. Our platform did the once-grueling work of identifying parts and material sources, comparing prices, factoring in geography, and considering tariffs. We lightened their mental load to allow them to make the best possible decisions about the parts they needed for their EV charging stations to minimize costs while maintaining quality. It has granted additional capacity to their small but mighty sourcing team to strategize for the next wave of growth they're positioned to experience.

A second underdog story I love comes from a home security company. This was a market that was largely dominated by ADT and Brinks for many years. How do you break into an industry against Goliath companies with strong brand awareness? This underdog realized that they couldn't get in the game by playing the same way that ADT and Brinks were. There was a high-cost barrier to entry with equipment, networks, and call centers. Additionally, consumers tended toward the trusted names to protect their homes and personal safety. A no-name brand wasn't going to cut it.

Our home security client realized that if they wanted to compete, they would have to reinvent the home security game. Rather than trying to appeal to the customers that their Goliath competitors already had, they went after a new segment of the market—one that found the ADT and Brinks way of doing things to be costly and cumbersome. They believed there was a customer base that craved simplicity and customization to their unique needs and fears. And like the ease of a video baby monitor, they wanted to empower their customers to have access and alerts to their own security footage without requiring them to sign up for expensive data storage.

To enter the market, they needed to compete on price and prove that they had a reliable system that worked. That's when they came to us. They understood the critical role that their sourcing function played in getting the parts they needed to produce consistent quality products at a price that was acceptable for the consumer base they were targeting. The LevaData platform not only allowed them to save on the current products they offered but also allowed them to more accurately predict pricing and lead times on potential future products. They had better data to decide what products were worth offering and which ones would not land at a price point where their customer base saw the value in them. This helped them excel in the present and continues to guide them towards smarter future products.

Our third client underdog is in the routing and switching networking industry, a market dominated by industry giants of the '80s and '90s, like Cisco and Juniper Networks. Our customer entered the market by focusing on being really good at supply chain management. They knew their technology and price were important but recognized that through supply chain management they could better manage their price and get their product to market. They succeeded in part because they recognized very early on that sourcing was their way to gain a competitive advantage.

They understood what big companies in their industry faced when it came to storing, managing, and interpreting data. Their timing was everything. Had they arrived on the market a decade or two prior, they would have been faced with the same data challenges the Goliaths of their industry were contending with. Instead, they were fortunate enough to come along at a time when there are enough robust tools to support them and their data.

Having the tools, like LevaData's platform, to contextualize their data and make intelligent, data-driven decisions helped them focus their spending and their labor on the things that mattered most. They were and continue to be a company with a data-first mindset. They didn't make a decision and then try to back it up with data; they worked the other way around. Data dictated action. Their data-first strategy using LevaData's tools allowed them to collate data across siloed systems to see and analyze their data in one place. Doing so helped them reduce risk and reveal hidden insights. Like a skilled fighter, they made calculated movements to find and maintain their footing.

While each of these companies has yet to take down the Goliath in their industry, they are still very much in the competition and continue gaining market share. We helped them do that through making their sourcing teams heroes within the supply chain. Our clients understand that COGS is a competitive advantage. If you can price your product lower and have a great profit margin, you can gain market share on the incumbent players. Our clients see opportunities to be different, use those differences as leverage, and act on them. That takes courage to step boldly into the arena and know which way you have to move to have a fighting chance.

The most crucial action a company can take is to acknowledge its limitations. This is no easy feat. We have employees who depend on us, investors and stakeholders who place their trust in us, and a compensation system that rewards success rather than the proactive avoidance of failure. However, failing to admit our shortcomings trades short-term comfort for long-term repercussions. We must cease deferring today's challenges to our future selves.

Why do we set ourselves up for future failure? Katy Milkman, professor at the Wharton School at the University of Pennsylvania and author of the book *How to Change*, attributes some of the reason to our "present bias." She has found that our long-term objectives and our short-term impulses are often not in alignment. Our present bias often means that we will apply a greater weight to choices that create an immediate reward and put less emphasis on things that have a long-term reward. For someone working in sourcing, I understand the desire to stay the course with the spreadsheets and emails that have served them for years. They know how they work, and they know what success looks like in that role. Why learn something new—especially if it means changing how they work or taking on different priorities?

The truth is, I have yet to find any magical words that can help people overcome their own present bias. Most people do not like to change and only reserve it for moments when they have no other choice. When I am faced with a change that feels too big, I look at what things will not change. If you're a sourcing professional bringing in the LevaData application, it won't change the fact that you will still have to exercise your keen contract negotiation skills. What will change is that you'll be backed with more quality data as leverage to negotiate. What won't change is that you will still have to build and maintain relationships with your suppliers. What will change is that you will be able to provide them greater data insights on the market landscape, which may help their own business. What won't change is your need to work with other departments within your organization. What will change is that you'll have a data dashboard as a single source of truth to make better decisions for the company as a whole. And that ever-present, hair-on-fire feeling that there is always a sourcing crisis to solve? The only way for that to change is if you're bold enough to make a real change in the way you and your department work.

You would likely be unsurprised to learn that one of my other favorite books is *The Wave: In Pursuit of the Rogues, Freaks, and Giants of the Ocean* by Susan Casey. The book opens with forty-seven scientists and a crew aboard the RRS Discovery in the icy seas off the coast of Scotland as they are pummeled by a mammoth hundred-foot wave. Casey goes on to explore stories from around the world—battles of human-kind and aquatic nature in seemingly insurmountable conditions. She includes historic voyages, from that of Ernest Shackleton crossing to Antarctica in 1916 to a renowned big wave surfer of the 1990s and 2000s, Laird Hamilton. Each story highlights a person or crew who never should have been able to do what they did. Each wave was one that defied scientific laws or was deemed an anomaly.

I found her stories of Laird Hamilton to be particularly intriguing. It's difficult to comprehend what it must have felt like to come up against some of these giants of the ocean. You are literally looking death in the face. I consider myself courageous in many ways, but Laird seemed to take it to a whole different level. It made me wonder why we all acted so differently. Why was my threshold for risk and change greater than some of the people around me? Why was Laird's threshold beyond what most humans would opt to face? And why were some people absolutely terrified or simply content with not taking risks or changing at all? So much of it seems to do with opportunity and mindset.

Laird grew up in Hawaii and was an exceptional surfer by the age of seventeen. Perhaps his tolerance for fear and risk came from facing them long before his prefrontal cortex had fully developed to alert him to choose otherwise. Regardless of the reason behind Laird's way of living, his philosophy on life has continued to propel him forward into new opportunities in both the sports and business world. He once said, "For those searching for something more than just the norm.

We lay it all down, including what others call sanity, for just a few moments on waves larger than life. We do this because we know there is still something greater than all of us. Something that inspires us spiritually. We start going downhill when we stop taking risks."

Laird wasn't just a surfer; he was an innovator in the field. He saw that certain types of waves couldn't be conquered through the surf methods at that time. Laird could have been content with being a really great surfer on the same waves that everyone else was riding. Instead, he developed new ways of doing things, like stand-up paddling and hydrofoiling, which further expanded the possibilities within surfing. Laird could have been great. He opted for legendary.

To become a hero of the supply chain, there are four key things to understand. First, you must be willing to make data a priority in the way you think and the way you operate. It cannot be a support or an afterthought. Data is *the* primary driver of your sourcing action. Secondly, you know how to leverage that data as your competitive advantage in the marketplace. Leveraging data can help mitigate risk factors, making your business more resilient through supply chain shocks.

The third thing to becoming a hero of the supply chain is to care about your COGS. You have to care more than wanting to save whatever percentage will help you look good on your annual performance review. You have to care like each cent that goes out the door, exponentiated over hundreds, thousands, or millions of transactions makes a difference. Every opportunity for savings matters.

Lastly, you become a hero of the supply chain because you take action when the time is right. We are at a real inflection point in the world of technology with the rapid adoption and incorporation of AI into business. But it's like the old adage, "You can lead a horse to water but you can't make it drink." Companies have to decide what they are going to do with the new technology available to them. Those with a strong culture of change will more easily adapt.

At LevaData, we are driven by the art of the possible. Our vision extends beyond the present, always looking towards the horizon to ensure that both we and our customers are ready for the next wave of opportunities. We are not looking to change how sourcing works, but we are always seeking possibilities to make sourcing more efficient and impactful for their companies. Like Laird when it came to the waves people said were unrideable, we don't walk away from the seemingly impossible challenge of the Data Gulch; we innovate. LevaData turns data into action in the modern supply chain. If you're ready to say goodbye to the frustration and confusion of the Decision Abyss, welcome aboard. It's time to be a sourcing hero.

CONCLUSION

The Surfer's Mindset

There is an irony to the title of this book, *Conquering the Decision Abyss*. Like the great waters I have referenced throughout the story, the Decision Abyss is not actually something that can ever be fully conquered. I know. "How anticlimactic of you, Keith." The reality is that it is virtually impossible to synthesize all the data available to make buying decisions. The LevaData platform provides you with the best possible options using the most data sources available, however, the technology does not make the decision for you. You still need to choose.

That means getting the departments within your organization to align on common goals. If you've ever sat in a planning meeting for a company event and tried to pick the menu that will please the most people, then you have felt the pain of trying to get unique parties with unique needs to come to a consensus. So long as you're working at a non-federated organization, where upper management or HR policies incentivize in ways that prioritize individual wins over company wins, there will always be a divide when it comes to choosing what is truly best.

If the Decision Abyss is unconquerable, unsolvable, and the Data Gulch is refilling with new data every day, then why do we even bother trying? Two simple answers: 1) because it's worth it; and 2) because we don't have another option. Manufacturing is entering a new sink-or-swim era in which companies, particularly the smaller, newer, or more agile ones, have an opportunity to expand their market share simply by staying ahead of the wave. That means making strategic investments where every dollar is spent with intentionality. That intentionality is driven by data intelligence. The companies that become the winners of the supply chain are those who are fishing with a spear rather than casting a wide net and hoping they pull in something they want. Know what you want. Know what matters. Go after it.

That still doesn't address the fact that it may feel defeating to even attempt to conquer something like the Decision Abyss. It may feel like a fool's journey. What can we do to keep ourselves engaged in such a necessary but endless endeavor? For that, I recommend following what is known as the Surfer's Mindset.

If you meet me, an Irish guy in a button-down shirt with a bit of a midwestern accent, in a boardroom, at a trade show, or on a Zoom call, it's unlikely that you'd pick me out as the surfing type. That's fair. But talk to me for a few minutes and you may learn that I've been an avid surfer for over two decades. I love the water and have both a deep respect and wonder for the way it works. In all my years of education and business, I still find that some of the most profound lessons I've learned about life have come from riding the waves.

Being a surfer means trying to find some predictability in the unpredictable. If you have education and experience to draw from, it is likely that you will fare better when a wave behaves differently than anticipated. But even the most seasoned surfers can find themselves in trouble if they let carelessness or pride get in their way. The more I work in the realm of sourcing, the more I realize it's not so different from surfing.

A while back I wrote a blog about the Surfer's Mindset. It was an exercise in identifying the lessons I've learned from the waves and articulating how they serve me in life. They provide a framework not only for how I problem-solve or approach new opportunities, but for how I should proceed when I'm feeling overwhelmed or stuck on a project. Life's challenges bring me back to memories of being crushed under a wave and dashed to the bottom, uncontrollably tumbling as helplessly as shells and sand. That's when I remember that the Surfer's Mindset has taught me to go with the water and not fight against it. Eventually, the wave subsides, and I'll be back on my board riding the next one.

If you have experienced the thrill of hitting the drop on a wave just right and riding to shore, it is infectious. It is such an exhilarating experience that you're willing to wipe out many more times for the chance to hit the drop and feel the energy of riding a wave once again. It's a big reason why I'm the guy who runs toward challenges in business. I've felt the excitement of solving the problems that others threw up their hands at in frustration. While I certainly can't fix everything, I am not afraid to try. I know that in the times where me and my teams can figure something out, make something better, or find a new way forward we get that same supercharged energy.

The Surfer's Mindset has served me in so many things that I do. It's a style of thinking that I strive to bring into everything

I do. I want to share it with you here in hope that you also find the value in it too, whether in your business or in your everyday life. There is so much that we can learn from nature.

Mindset 1: Get in the water
if you want to ride the waves

It's comfortable to watch surfing from the shore. I've seen many people stand there in their wetsuits, board in hand, observing the surfers riding and getting taken down by the waves while trying to build up their nerves to enter the water. Surfing can be scary, and that first step is the hardest.

The reality of surfing is that all surfers know that, at some point, they are going to wipe out. It's inevitable, even for the greats out there. But regardless of how the water treats them, surfers always paddle back out and try again. Mistakes are part of the process. In fact, it would be foolish to expect that you could surf *without* wiping out. We use our mistakes and our wipeouts to make us stronger and smarter. It's a bit of trial and error to learn what works for us. We get a little bit better every day and a little bit better week after week, month after month.

Procurement and direct material sourcing is the same way. There's a fear of getting started in new ways of working. It's the fear of the new way not working out or not working fast enough. But the thing is, others are doing it. There are companies out there who are Laird Hamilton-ing it right now in the sourcing realm. We can see the success of others who have decided to work differently and would never go back to their old ways. Even Laird has to start with a first step, though. You have to be willing to put one foot on the board and try.

MINDSET 2: CREATE A STRATEGIC POSITION WHEN YOU'RE ABOUT TO BE CRUSHED BY A WAVE

There is nothing quite like the feeling of impending doom as you realize you're about to be crushed by a wave. There isn't anything you can do to stop that wave—it was never in your control to begin with. What you can control is your reaction, though. You can position yourself to maneuver through the wave without allowing it to suck you back into the ocean's depths. You will feel the impact of the wave, but being proactive in your preparation can often lessen your pain and get you back on your feet faster.

Even still, I see surfers who realize they're about to be crushed by a wave and they panic. While they're often inexperienced surfers, some are also people who never think to try differently. To them, the panic followed by the crush and the feelings of drowning are part of their surf experience. They don't think to ask questions. They don't look for new ways to recover. They lather, rinse, repeat in the same unfortunate cycle, assuming that panic and pain are an inevitable part of what surfing is. I find that these people generally don't stick with surfing for very long.

Strategic positioning in sourcing is crucial to surviving supply chain shocks as well. There's no doubt that the coming years will bring new crushing challenges to the supply chain. Procurement teams can position themselves as value drivers, contributing directly to the bottom lines of their organizations, if they have the tools to do so. AI-powered insights can't keep supply shocks from happening, but they can provide advance notice so teams can pivot on parts and suppliers before supply shifts affect customers. When we know how to recover, when we go in with a plan, those crushing waves become less scary and less damaging.

MINDSET 3: ONLY RIDE THE BEST WAVES
INSTEAD OF REACTING TO EVERY WAVE

In my early surfing days, a surf instructor told me to look out at the ocean and focus on a wave. I watched it swell into a crescendo, the crest turning white as it curled over the deepening trough below before rolling forward and crashing down on itself before it dissipated back into the flow of the water. My instructor asked me to look at another wave and I watched it do the same. Then I observed another wave, and another. They varied in size and timing. Some looked clean and picturesque while others seemed to fizzle out or roll in anticlimactically. "What did you notice?" he asked. I paused for a moment, my mind filling with a myriad of answers but not knowing exactly what he was looking for. He filled in the blank. "The waves don't stop. One comes in and there are many more behind it. Not every wave is worth a ride."

This was a valuable lesson as a novice. Not every wave is catchable. Not every wave is worth our energy or reaction. Becoming a great surfer means learning to know when it's time to catch one and when it's time to wait. It makes us strategic in how we spend our time and energy for the most satisfying result.

This too is mirrored in sourcing. What if you could learn how to spot the biggest spending opportunities right now? Or what if you could get a benchmark for a custom part that's otherwise un-benchmarkable? Rather than years of training, you have access to AI-powered intelligence that can help you identify the biggest and best ways to manage spend and risk so you can prioritize the most valuable opportunities instead of reacting once things change. You can stop racing after what doesn't really matter so that you have the time and energy to focus on what does.

MINDSET 4: LEARN FROM PAST FAILURES

It's not easy to pop up on a surfboard and catch a wave at first. There is a lot that goes into having a good day on the waves. There are surfers who choose the wrong board. A board that's too small for your weight or skill level will make it hard to paddle into waves while a board that's too large can be cumbersome and slow. As someone new, it's not always easy to determine if the tools we're using are not right. We haven't yet figured out how it's supposed to feel, which is why we work with more experienced surfers to improve our attunement to board problems.

Some novice surfers, bless their ambitious hearts, seem to feel an irrational pull toward wanting to tackle a monster wave far before they're ready. Maybe they spent too much time watching movies like *Point Break* or *Blue Crush* and believe that once they've taken on a few waves, they can take on *any* wave. Hollywood has led them astray and they quickly learn that the ocean is a harsh teacher.

Master surfers are continually learning from their mistakes. With each wipeout they assess what went wrong and how they could respond differently. The mindset of "This is what I've always done, and this is how I do it" doesn't work when it comes to the water. It's unpredictable, but it does follow some patterns. A surfer's job is not to remain rigid and hope (fruitlessly) that the water will adapt to them. The best surfers are the ones who embrace the known unpredictability of the waves and learn from them.

If procurement teams have learned anything over the past several years, it's that the somewhat unpredictable nature of demand shocks cannot be managed with traditional procurement processes and tools. This is another place where our rigidity and adherence to ways that have caused problems in the past, creates future issues. It's the forward-thinking organizations that embody the mindset of the expert surfer and embracing the knowledge of AI for their direct material sourcing. Not only do AI-powered insights unearth incredible new value for the company but they also enable procurement teams to learn about and avoid potential failures.

MINDSET 5: COMMIT

One of the biggest fears for new surfers is what is known as "the drop." It is the transition from paddling to standing that has to occur at just the right time to ride a wave. The drop can be studied, but it is best learned through repetition and experience.

Surfers fear the drop for a variety of reasons. Maybe their knees aren't in the greatest shape anymore or they're worried about their balance. I think even more of the fear comes from having to take decisive action with whatever information, education, or experience you have. Hitting the drop in surfing is only as effective as your level of commitment to it. You can't spend time with a foot in both worlds, so to speak. Move half-heartedly and you're headed for a wipeout. Hesitate and the wave has passed you by.

One way to overcome this fear of the drop is by practicing on dry land. In nearly all surf lessons I've taken and observed, there is a period where the instructor will go through the motions. The new surfer gets to practice and get comfortable with the feel of the movement of transitioning from paddling to standing. They repeat the movement over and over to build muscle memory, but more importantly to help lessen the surfer's fear. Fear is not the dominant emotion you want to lead you through any important event.

It's the same way that we guide our customers through a test run of using the LevaData system with their own data. Me, putting graphics on a slide deck from some other company and saying, "*Voila!* See how easy it's done?" would be the equivalent of my surf instructor showing me a clip of Laird Hamilton and saying, "You just need to copy that guy!" That's not how it works.

When we experience it for ourselves, we learn better. We realize what questions we need to ask. We identify potential issues (like a shaky knee or a gap in our data) that might need to be addressed before we commence. Having that ability to practice on the safety of dry land greatly improves our ability to enter the water successfully.

Like learning to spot and commit to taking the drop on the perfect wave, teams that use AI to transform their direct material sourcing can spot opportunities in real time, adding millions to the company's bottom line. When the opportunity to immediately transform your supply chain utilizing AI-powered insights presents itself, it's time to jump in and commit.

So much of surfing is about being in the right place at the right time and with the right energy to paddle. It's also about claiming your wave. It's highly likely that you're not the only surfer in the water. Everyone is vying for that perfect wave. If you want it, you have to beat them to it, paddling and hitting the drop at precisely the right time. You have to be hungry for it. Isn't that so much of how we experience success in other areas of our lives?

In sourcing, you have to have the right parts at the right price for you to assemble, ship, and sell. It's a million tiny decisions, timings, and efforts that go into hitting the equivalent of "the drop" in manufacturing. You have to decide when to commit, or you let opportunities pass you by. When sourcing teams hit this drop, it's an incredible thing to witness their success.

Everything seems to flow. It's hard to watch the opposite, when teams wipe out.

I am always on the lookout for the underdogs, whether it's the determined new surfer who just needs to try a different board or stance, or the small but high-growth company that needs more efficient ways to work to keep going. These entities already possess greatness, but like everyone else, they can't improve alone. My goal is to assist them, just as many have helped me throughout my life.

Navigating the Decision Abyss may seem unconquerable. However, with the right guidance and tools, you can significantly improve your journey across it and actually enjoy the journey too.

If we could tame the seas, we would never experience the joy and gratification that comes from navigating them. Similarly, the challenges in sourcing are what make the successes so fulfilling. When someone catches a wave, it's the most beautiful thing in the world—just like finding the perfect solution in sourcing.

ACKNOWLEDGMENTS

Writing a book is never a solitary endeavor, and I am deeply grateful to the many people who have supported me along the way. This journey has been one of growth, reflection, and grit, and I owe a great deal to those who stood by me through every chapter—both literal and metaphorical.

First and foremost, I want to thank my wife Bryn. Your unwavering belief in me has been the cornerstone of this entire project. Your patience, encouragement, and quiet strength have carried me through long nights and early mornings. You've been my sounding board, my editor, my cheerleader, and my voice of reason. This book would not exist without your love and support, and I am endlessly grateful for the life we've built together.

To my children—Elsa and Mikaela—you are my greatest inspiration. Your curiosity, resilience, and boundless energy remind me every day of the importance of storytelling and the power of imagination. You make me laugh out loud, and remind me daily of what truly matters. I hope this book shows you that dreams are worth chasing (just like the bigger, gnarlier waves!), even when the path is long and winding.

I am also deeply thankful to my mom and dad. Your love and steadfast support laid the foundation for everything I've accomplished. You taught me the value of hard work, integrity, and kindness. I carry your lessons with me everywhere.

To my in-laws: thank you for welcoming me into your family. You introduced me to sailing and construction, and I will always be grateful for the education. So many of my favorite stories and lessons have happened with you; I always feel like a student in your presence.

I also want to extend my heartfelt thanks to the many former employers and bosses who played a pivotal role in shaping my professional journey. Each of you, in your own way, contributed to the person and writer I've become. To those who challenged me—you pushed me to grow. To those who mentored me—you taught me the value of guidance and generosity. And to those who believed in me—you gave me the confidence to grow as a leader.

LevaData started in the brain of Rajesh Kalidindi, who founded LevaData with the sole mission of helping direct material sourcing professionals. Rajesh courageously entrusted the LevaData mission to me, and I am grateful for his encouragement and support.

The team of Aaron Fleishman and Sheila Gulati at Tola Capital realized the potential of what LevaData could provide in the market. They invested more than money; their time and energy is the model for how investors should behave and act with their portfolio companies.

To the Banneker Partners team of Kenny Frank, Terrance Bei, and Harjot Sachdeva: thank you for the camaraderie, support, and experiences you have shared. My perspective has been enriched, and your diversity of thought has deeply influenced my thinking and leadership. You set the bar high on dimensions of integrity, honesty and trust, and any company would be fortunate to have your voice on their Board of Directors.

I was thrilled to have Angel Mendez write the forward to this book. Angel is a supply chain legend, and I am honored to call him a mentor, coach, and friend. Angel, you always keep my eye on the horizon for the next set of waves approaching (thank you for that!).

A huge shout out to my literary team who kept me on track and offered timely suggestions, encouragement, and just the right dose of pull to my push. Jill Abby, you are a rock star, and I am forever grateful to have collaborated on this book with you.

To my colleagues and friends from LevaData: every day I consider myself the most fortunate CEO on Earth, working with such a diversely talented and passionate group of professionals. I am in awe of the things we are doing together to serve sourcing professionals, and believe the best is still to come.

Finally, to the readers: the supply chain and sourcing nerds, who quite literally spend their lives making products for the world to consume. I am one of you. Thank you for picking up this book and giving it your time and attention. I hope it resonates with you, challenges you, or simply brings you a moment of joy and (hopefully) laughter. I am honored to share these pages with you.

Carpe Punctum,

Keith

ABOUT KEITH HARTLEY

Keith Hartley is a seasoned technology executive, board advisor, and global supply chain thought leader with over twenty-five years of experience driving growth and transformation for enterprise software companies. He currently serves as CEO and board member of LevaData, an AI-powered supply management platform that helps companies optimize direct material sourcing through predictive, actionable insights.

Keith is also the founder of The Abyss Group, an advisory firm that helps companies architect and scale transformative go-to-market strategies. Through his work at The Abyss Group, he works with clients on understanding the Data Gulch and how to conquer their Decision Abyss.